HEAVEN IN STONE AND GLASS

Robert Barron

HEAVEN IN STONE AND GLASS

EXPERIENCING THE SPIRITUALITY OF THE GREAT CATHEDRALS

A Crossroad Book
The Crossroad Publishing Company
New York

The Crossroad Publishing Company
481 Eighth Avenue, Suite 1550
New York, NY 10001

Printed in the United States of America

Library of Congress Cataloging-in-Publication Data
Barron, Robert E., 1959-
    Heaven in stone and glass : experiencing the spirituality of the
    great cathedrals / by Robert Barron.
        p.   cm.
    Includes bibliographical references.
    ISBN 0-8245-1863-2 (alk. paper)
    1. Cathedrals – France – Meditations.   I. Title.
BX4629.A1 B37 2000
246'.96'0944 – dc21

00-008830

1   2   3   4   5   6   7   8   9   10   06   05   04   03   02   01   00

To the memory of
Fr. John Rose,
who loved the Gothic cathedrals
and who has now taken his place
in the heavenly liturgy

Contents

Illustrations

8

Acknowledgments

I would like to thank Gwendolin Herder, the publisher of Crossroad Publishing Company, who first suggested I write a book on the spirituality of the cathedrals and who has been a steady source of inspiration and encouragement. I would also like to express my gratitude to my good friend Fr. Stephen Grunow, who read the manuscript carefully and made very helpful suggestions and who, much more importantly, kept my mind clearly focused on the Christ who is the raison d'être of the cathedrals. Finally, I would like to thank Dr. Ewert Cousins, who loves the medieval mind and who has modeled for me the life of the prayerful scholar.

A Cathedral Must Be Read

I F WE ARE to appreciate the great cathedrals, we must move into the medieval mind. And this means that we must become comfortable with a relentlessly symbolic imagination. We, the heirs of the Enlightenment and the age of technology, have a prosaic cast of mind: we like our ideas clear and distinct, and we like our words direct and unambiguous. But to such a consciousness the cathedrals will remain stubbornly opaque, for they were produced by people for whom the whole world — animals, planets, insects, grasses, seas, and clouds — were symbolic manifestations of a spiritual universe that cannot be seen. That medieval people loved the ordinary things of this world is obvious. One can see it, for instance, in the detail of their illuminated manuscripts and carvings. But for them the beauties of this universe were but a foretaste and shadow of the Beauty that created them, a veil transparent to the ultimately real.

Accordingly, everything in a Gothic cathedral produces a tone and then a variety of overtones evocative

11

of a transcendent harmony. And everything in a
Gothic cathedral tells a story which in turn opens
onto the narrative being spun by God. Our problem is that we are largely deaf to those overtones
and largely clueless with regard to the great story.
Therefore we must learn once again how to hear and
to read these buildings. We must train ourselves to
perform the hermeneutic that medieval people ex-
ercised spontaneously and naturally: understanding
the cathedral as an icon of the sacred, a bearer of the
mystery of God. One of the serious problems that
we face is that for the past thirty years this iconic
element has been undervalued. Our church buildings
have become largely empty spaces, void of imagery
and color, places where the people gather but not
places that, themselves, tell a story.

But why am I bothering with this exercise at all?
Why is it important to recover the medieval imagination so that we can enter into the mysteries of these
old buildings? It is vital because these cathedrals are
powerful repositories of the Christian spirit, vehicles
of the new being that became available in Jesus of
Nazareth. In their windows, towers, vaults, naves,
roses, labyrinths, altars, and façades, these Gothic
churches bring the transformative energy of Jesus
Christ to bear on our world. In a spiritually hungry
time, I think that the cathedrals can do what they
have always done for those who are open: teach the

faith and focus the journey of the spirit. St. Augustine said that the mind curiously delights in a truth that comes in an indirect and symbolically evocative way. The cathedrals teach the truth of Christ in precisely this delightfully indirect manner. To be honest, I write this book especially for my generation of Christians, who came of age in a rather iconoclastic time and who hence never developed the eye or mind to read a church. I will endeavor to reveal some treasures that became unavailable to many younger believers.

Taking as their inspiration the story of Jesus healing the blind man, many of the Fathers of the Church said that Christ himself is a sort of "salve" for eyes blinded by sin. Through his power and presence, we are able to see the world aright. The cathedrals, as embodiments and expressions of Christ, constitute a way of seeing, an avenue to another world. It is this coming to see that I would like to explore. What I will do then, in a series of meditations, is to take as a starting point some aspect of a Gothic cathedral and then read it symbolically, showing the spiritual world to which it is transparent. With you, I will walk around the cathedrals at a slow pace and in a meditative frame of mind, letting their mysteries emerge. Together we will make a pilgrimage.

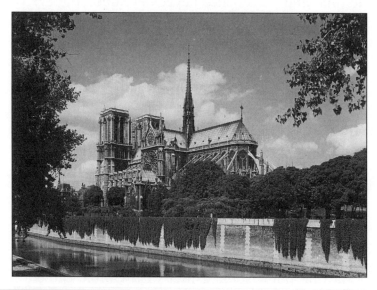

Notre-Dame, Paris, France. View from the southeast.
(Foto Marburg/Art Resource, NY)

1

Notre-Dame

A LMOST ALL of the great Gothic cathedrals of France are dedicated to *Notre-Dame,* our Lady. In the centuries prior to the Gothic period, Christian churches were named for a variety of saints, but from the end of the twelfth and into the thirteenth century the cathedrals were, almost without exception, named for the Virgin. Oceans of ink have been spilled trying to explain this phenomenon of Mary's sudden prominence, and I will not add another theory. Suffice it to say, the great cavernous cathedrals of the Middle Ages were seen, in an almost literal sense, as the body of Mary, places of safety and birth. I can testify that, standing in the midst of Chartres, Amiens, or Notre-Dame de Paris, one feels an overwhelming sense of security, a peacefulness and serenity of spirit. The dark, all-enveloping space is evocative of the womb in which Christ himself was nurtured and in which all members of the church come to birth.

From the earliest centuries, the church was referred to as "mother," *mater ecclesia,* and Mary, the mother of Jesus, was closely associated with it as its symbol, protector, and premier member. Catholic theologian Hans Urs von Balthasar says that, in her total acceptance of the will of God, her "yes" without qualification or hesitation, Mary becomes the matrix of the Christian community, the spiritual space in which all of our positive responses to God find their home. And therefore her attitude of acquiescence to God's designs *is* the safety which is the church.

When the pilgrims came to Chartres, they were hoping to see a most holy relic, the *chemise* (the tunic) of the Virgin, but at a deeper level they were seeking security, and it was this spiritual rest that they found in the womb of the cathedral and the embrace of the Virgin. Now there is nothing easy or cheap about this repose offered by Mary, and they knew it. All over the cathedrals are depictions of the Annunciation, Mary's "yes," but there are also vivid reminders of all that flowed from that acceptance: the massacre of the innocents, the flight into Egypt, the awful vigil at the foot of the cross. The peace realized and embodied by Mary is not the peace that the world gives, but rather the serenity beyond pleasure and pain that follows from an acceptance of our role in God's dramatic designs.

This theme of safety and rest is also evoked in the name given to the central section of the cathedral:

the nave. The etymology of the word is somewhat ambiguous, but it seems to be derived from the Latin *navis,* meaning ship or boat. Medieval people knew — perhaps even more vividly than we — that human life is a dangerous proposition. We are surrounded on all sides by threats: warfare, disease, failure, economic collapse, loss of friendship, death itself. Paul Tillich said that the basic human emotion is fear because "finitude in awareness is anxiety." Our time on earth is like the disciples' anxious journey across the stormy sea of Galilee. We are so often swamped, beset, convinced that death is near. But in the boat with the disciples was Christ, incongruously asleep. The sleeping Jesus stands, the Church Fathers tell us, for that place of safety and peace that is available even in the worst storms, that still-point of God's grace in the tumult of a human life. As long as we are rooted in the divine power of Christ, nothing can finally overwhelm us. The old Quaker hymn expresses this confidence: "No storm can shake my inmost calm, while to that rock I'm clinging...."

And so the church, the place where Christ dwells, is our shelter in the storm, our land of peace. When pilgrims enter the hull of this cathedral-ship, they are meant to feel a rush of relief, a keen sensation of being secure even as the waves crash against the vessel. The early Church Father Origen of Alexandria inaugurated a long tradition of identifying the church of Jesus Christ with the Ark of Noah. In the midst of the storms and floods of sin, the church is that boat (the barque of Peter) where the chosen people find their surety. The strong sides of Noah's ark, covered with pitch both inside and out, stand for the teachers and defenders of the faith; the variety of the animals signifies the multiplicity of those who are saved; the different levels of the ark speak of the varying degrees of spiritual attainment possible within the church.

If you position yourself behind Notre-Dame Cathedral in Paris and look back at the mighty building as it looms over the Seine, you see the flying buttresses jutting out from the side of the church. And with this naval imagery in mind, you can't help but imagine them as oars sticking out from a great ship and propelling it through the ages. The illusion is encouraged, of course, by the fact that Notre-Dame sits on the Île de la Cité, an island in the middle of the Seine.

The interior space of the church, the body of Notre-Dame, is therefore a place of safety, but it is also, as I suggested above, a womb, a place of gestation and birth. The purpose of the church is not merely to keep us safe from the dangers of the world; it is to bring us to fullness of life. St. Irenaeus suggested that Adam and Eve in the Garden of

Eden were not so much full-fledged adults as adolescents — somewhat unsure of themselves, testing their freedom — and that the whole history of salvation is a long, sometimes tortuous, process of development and education, God cajoling his people in the direction of salvation. According to this vision, the church is that place where the growth, the education, the gestation of the race continues. Our life here below, lived out in the nurturing confines of the church, is like the development of the fetus in the womb.

Now to be sure, a womb is a place of safety and comfort, but it is not the proper or final environment for the child. In fact, as the baby grows within her mother, she becomes increasingly uncomfortable, preparing for the moment when she will emerge into the spacious and colorful world for which she is destined. So we gestate in the womb of the mother-cathedral, taking in the nourishment of her stories, pictures, and doctrines, and growing, year by year, uncomfortable with this world, readying ourselves for the far richer, broader, and more beautiful world which God is preparing for us. Wombs are secure, but they are not our final home; ships are safe, but they are taking us somewhere.

Chartres Cathedral, France. (Foto Marburg/Art Resource, NY)

2

Light and Darkness

WHEN ONE ENTERS a Gothic cathedral, one is plunged into darkness. As the eyes struggle to adjust from the relative brightness outside to the dimness of the interior, one is practically blinded. During my time in France, I often witnessed the phenomenon of people stumbling and groping helplessly as they passed through the portals of a cathedral. The difficulty comes, not only from the natural incapacity of the eyes, but from the fact that the darkest portion of the interior is precisely near the main doors. None of this, of course, is by accident.

The Gothic architects wanted to impress something of terrible spiritual moment upon the minds of those who visited the cathedrals: we are a people who walk in darkness. Two basic assumptions of the Christian spiritual teachers across the ages are that we are sinners and that we find it very easy to overlook that fact. Christianity is a salvation religion: it assumes that there is something dreadfully wrong with us and that we require God's grace to solve our problem. When Jesus opens his mouth for the first time in Mark's Gospel he says, "The Kingdom of God is at hand; repent and believe the good news." His inaugural address is therefore a call to conversion, to a radical change of heart, mind, vision, and direction. If all were well with us, there would be no need to change, and if we could save ourselves, we would not need a deliverer to come to us from the outside.

The problem, recognized by Christian teachers from St. John the Evangelist to Flannery O'Connor, is that we pretend we are not sinners, we become blind to our blindness. Often the most important step in our spiritual development is an awakening to just how lost we are. Dante's *Divine Comedy* opens with the line: "Midway on the journey of our life I awoke to find myself alone and lost in a dark wood, having wandered from the straight path." Dante's adventure of the spirit, which will take him from Hell to Purgatory to Heaven, can begin only when he wakes from a slumber of complacency and self-righteousness, only when he comes to the painful realization that he stands in need of grace.

Saul of Tarsus was utterly convinced that he was doing the will of God as he rode off to persecute the infant church in Damascus. He grasped that he was in fact going in precisely the wrong direction only when he was addressed by Jesus and blinded by his divine light. The climax of Flannery O'Connor's short story "Revelation" occurs when Mrs. Turpin, a Christian woman sure of her own moral superiority, hears the words spoken to her by a disheveled and disagreeable young woman: "You are a wart-hog from hell!" That unpleasant but brutally honest accuser, by the way, is named "Mary-Grace." The breakthrough of God's grace is sometimes a harsh and dreadful thing, especially when it cracks open the defensive shell of our self-righteousness. So the Gothic cathedral, full of the power of Christ, does not allow us to wallow in the illusion of our sinlessness. We may enter the door with confidence, sure of our direction and purpose, but the moment we step into the cathedral, we are disoriented, lost, desperately in need of a guide.

What is wonderful is that the cathedral itself emerges as that guide. Just as Christ blinded Saul and then sent him help in the person of Ananias, so the cathedral casts us into the shadows and then shows us the light. As we move through the church — with hesitation at first — we come to ever greater illumination, the windows allowing more and more light into the space. The spiritual lesson is clear: as long as we sinners stay in the confines of the church, we will make our way to the Light; when we try to walk outside the church, our blindness only intensifies.

To speak of the light in Gothic cathedrals is to come nearly to the heart of the matter. In his first

letter, St. John summed up the Christian experience in these words: "God is light; in him there is no darkness." Ever since, Christian theologians, spiritual teachers, and saints have been fascinated by the metaphor of light. Beautiful, evanescent, all-embracing, in itself invisible but that which allows things to be seen, light seems to be the perfect symbol for the alluring, creating, omnipresent but finally elusive God. Romanesque architects wanted to illumine their buildings, but they couldn't find a way to open great spaces for windows without inordinately weakening the walls that held up the vault. One of the strokes of genius that characterized Gothic architecture and that made brilliant illumination possible was the flying buttress, an external support that effectively took the enormous weight of the vault off the walls and carried it down to the ground. Taking the pressure off the walls enabled the architect to cut huge windows in them and thus to flood the interior with light. This Gothic space is thus a foretaste of the heavenly Jerusalem where, as the psalmist says, "in your light we will see light." Having stumbled in, the pilgrim now sees.

Christians know something of God from sources philosophical, mythological, historical, and poetic, but their deepest grasp of the nature of God comes from Jesus of Nazareth, the Logos, the spoken Word of the Father. This Jesus was the friend of the marginalized, the healer of the disabled and the sick, the advocate of the forgotten, the forgiver of sins. His mission was to carry the fire of divine mercy to all those who were cut off from it. In doing so, he excited the wrath and opposition of the powerful, all those whose status depended upon an ideology of violence, differentiation, and exclusion. When he was born, "Herod and with him all Jerusalem" trembled, and when he came on the public scene, demons screamed and Pharisees schemed and protectors of the establishment plotted to do away with him. In the end, he was put to death by a conspiracy of the secular and religious authorities, and, in his moment of greatest danger, he was betrayed, denied, and abandoned by even his dearest friends. Jesus did not simply die; he was executed, eliminated, and he died precisely because of the way he lived.

But then he came back from the dead; the light that they put out shone again through the power of the Father: "the light shone in the darkness and the darkness could not overcome it." In the Gospel of Luke, we hear that the disciples, upon seeing the risen Christ, were terrified. I have always thought that this fear came, not just from the novelty of the event, but from the conviction that he was back for vengeance. As in a ghost story, the wronged victim seemed to have returned from the grave seeking revenge. But the risen Jesus reaches out to those who had abandoned him and says, simply, "Shalom," peace. In approaching his disciples in forgiveness and non-violence, Jesus shows that God is not only love for the victims, but also reconciliation for the victimizers. If he had returned in retribution, he would have represented the old myth of order through violence, God establishing justice through crushing the perpetrators of injustice. Instead, the resurrected Christ repudiates that myth and brands that god as an idol. The divine power is not love for some and hatred for others, not a friend of his own and an enemy of their enemies — rather, *God is love,* right through, with no qualification, no compromise, no question. As Jesus says in the Sermon on the Mount, "God makes his sun to shine on the good and the bad alike, and his rain to fall on the just and the unjust." Unlike the gods of mythology and philosophy and popular belief, divinities who are both dark and light, the real God is light; "in him there is no darkness."

This conviction concerning the nature of God is hardly a mere theological precision; it opens up a new world. If God is love, if the very source and ground of existence is nothing but light, then our world, so characterized by the shadows of violence, hatred, retribution, and the inability to forgive, is itself a kind of illusion and shadow. And the church, which bears the power of the true God, is therefore the harbinger of a new society, the herald of a new way of being.

There is a wonderful description of the construction of Chartres Cathedral that has come down to us from the twelfth century. It says that people from all walks of life and social strata — lords, ladies, soldiers, and common workers — came together in the grueling task of transporting stones, wine, grain, and oil to the work site. They labored side by side and in reverential silence — and all forgave their enemies. What we see here is a hint of the new city made possible by the authority of the risen Christ at work in his church. When we visit a Gothic cathedral and move into the magnificent light of the place, it is the true God that we are meant to praise and this new world that we are compelled to imagine.

Chartres Cathedral, France. South Rose Window, 1224.
(Scala/Art Resource, NY)

3

Rose Windows

WHEN the nineteenth-century artist and restorer Eugène-Emmanuel Viollet-le-Duc was a child, his mother took him to Notre-Dame Cathedral in Paris. Captivated by the great rose in the north transept, the boy cried out, "Maman, écoute, c'est le rosace qui chante!" (Listen, Mama, it is the rose that is singing.) Many over the centuries who have stood in the presence of the Gothic rose windows have, I imagine, heard that same song, sensed that same lyricism. I can personally testify to the enchanting power of Gothic roses. When I was a student in Paris, I was drawn, almost compulsively, to gaze upon the same rose that entranced the young Viollet-le-Duc. I would stand before the window, in a kind of aesthetic arrest, for twenty or thirty minutes and always felt refreshed and enlivened after the experience. The play of light, color, harmony, and balance, all enveloped in the perfection of the circle, establishes an aesthetic energy which can, it seems, be described only in musical terms.

Why, of all of the features of the Gothic cathedral, do these flowers of color seem the most involving? Perhaps it is because they most fully embody what the medieval scholastics took to be *the* characteristics of the beautiful: *integritas* (wholeness), *consonantia* (harmony), and *claritas* (radiance). The philosophers of the Middle Ages felt that to be appreciated as beautiful, a thing must, first, be seen whole, in its entirety; it must be isolated from the rest of its environment. Second, it must be marked by a harmonious play of part against part, a kind of balanced rhythm. Finally, it must shine. If one or two of these qualities is present, a thing might be striking or arresting or interesting, but it is beautiful only when the three graciously intersect. Therefore, when the sunlight passes through the ordered and circumscribed arrangement of color that is the rose window, when this harmony becomes radiant, the beautiful, in an almost paradigmatic sense, appears.

And this beauty was, for the medieval world, far from trivial "prettiness," hardly a mere decorative trait. Rather, the beautiful, along with the good and the true, was seen as a transcendental property of being, that is to say, as one of the essential characteristics of existence. Whatever is, they thought, is good (because it is desirable), true (because it is knowable), and beautiful (because it captivates).

Therefore, all earthly beauty is a sign of the fullness of beauty, which belongs to God, the source and perfection of being. The especially arresting beauty of the rose window was meant as a sacrament and anticipation of the beatific vision of God's beauty that would occur at the end of time.

For the medieval theologians, heaven was a place of rest, but we must be careful lest we misconstrue this term. It has nothing to do with inactivity or indolence; it has everything to do with savoring, tasting, and active engagement. Thomas Aquinas says that the will has two basic acts: it seeks the good that it does not possess, and it *rests* in the good that it does possess. Thus one can seek to have a million dollars, but one rests in a good baseball game, an engaging conversation, a work of art. Heaven is *resting* in the beauty of God, that is, ecstatically appreciating it, being drawn totally out of oneself in the loving and tasting of it. In the presence of a beautiful person or thing, we are enraptured, literally taken out of ourselves, as was Joyce's Stephen Daedalus when he spied the lovely girl on the strand outside of Dublin. The beatific vision is the height of aesthetic arrest and spiritual ecstasy — and hence the summit of joy.

The theme of the beatific vision is highlighted in the north rose at Notre-Dame in Paris through the use of number symbolism. Around the center of the rose is a circle of eight images. Then, in succeeding rows, we find multiples of eight — sixteen and thirty-two — and the total number of images is eighty-eight. Thus the entire rose is a sustained meditation on the number eight. Now eight, coming just beyond seven, which is the symbol of completed time, stands for that dimension of reality that lies beyond time, that is, eternity. Thus the mystical message is clear: the fullness of beauty, vaguely hinted at in the rose, will become visible only when we pass beyond time into the eternal realm.

The Lord Jesus says, "if you want your life, lose it," and it is this wonderful loss of self that happens when we listen to the singing of the rose window.

The rose is also an evocative symbol of what the spirit masters refer to as the center. All rose windows have the same basic construction. At the center is, invariably, a depiction of Christ. If it seems as though Mary is at the heart of the window, we must look more closely and see that on her lap sits the Christ child. Then, wheeling around the Christic core is a harmoniously arranged amalgam of "medallions," pictures and images from the Scripture or the lives of the saints. The medallions are often connected to one another and ultimately to the center by a series of spokes. This structured harmony is intended to be a picture of the well-ordered soul. When the divine power is the uncompromised center of our

lives, then the myriad energies of our souls — intellectual, moral, physical, emotional, and sexual — tend to fall into harmony around it. When Christ is the "ground" of the soul, the soul finds peace, order, and beauty. And consequently, the window teaches us, when something other than Christ — money, power, prestige, sensual pleasure — becomes the center of our lives, our soul energies become disordered, dysfunctional, chaotic. Jesus said, "Seek ye first the Kingdom of God and his righteousness, and the rest shall be given unto you." In other words, make God's will the center of your concerns, and your proximate needs, desires, and longings will tend to find their place.

At the very beginning of Mark's Gospel, Jesus confronts a young man who is possessed by an unclean spirit. The demoniac shouts at him: "What do you want of *us,* Jesus of Nazareth? Have you come to destroy *us?*" Then later in the same Gospel, Jesus addresses the Gerasene demoniac: "What is your name?" And the answer comes: "Legion, for there are hundreds of *us.*" It is worthy of note how often the New Testament demons speak in the plural. They are those who have lost their center in God and who therefore have splintered and divided souls, speaking from one perspective and then another, tyrannized by one desire and then another, dominated by a succession of masters. When we lose our rootedness in the divine power, we too are split, riven, shattered. And we experience our inner lives as a cacophony of voices and a maelstrom of unintegrated drives.

There is a scene in the play *A Man for All Seasons* in which Thomas More tries to explain to his friend the Duke of Norfolk why he feels obliged to oppose Henry VIII's domination of the church, even when almost the entire leadership of England has given in. "I will not give in because I oppose it — I do — not my pride, not my spleen, nor any other of my appetites but *I* do...." Then, addressing Norfolk provocatively, he says, "Is there no single sinew in the midst of this that serves no appetite of Norfolk, just Norfolk? Give *that* some exercise, my lord!" Thomas More, serene even in his moment of greatest danger, is speaking from his deepest center, that still-point around which all of his "appetites" revolve and in which they find their purpose, and he is trying to awaken that same power in his spiritually compromised friend. The rose window is a picture of the properly centered soul. And this is another reason, I think, why meditating upon it is such a peaceful experience. Like a mandala or an icon, the rose window works a sort of psychological alchemy in those who gaze upon it, reordering their souls according to its pattern, as Jesus by the sheer power of his presence brought the demoniacs back to themselves.

There is another circle found in many of the Gothic cathedrals that makes much the same spiritual point as the rose window. This is the so-called wheel of fortune. In most depictions of the wheel, a great circle is topped by a crowned figure, and over his head is the word *regno* (I am reigning). Moving clockwise along the rim of the wheel, we come to a man who has lost his crown and is tumbling downward, and next to him is the word *regnavi* (I have reigned). At the bottom of the wheel is a pauper dressed in rags, and his motto is the sad phrase *sum sine regno* (I have no power). Finally, as we move upward on the left side of the circle, we come to an ambitious figure eagerly climbing to the top. And he says, *"regnabo"* (I will reign). At the center of the wheel of fortune, at the meeting point of the spokes, is the figure of Christ.

The spiritual lesson is simple and profound. Throughout one's life, the wheel of fortune turns, placing one sometimes in positions of power and pleasure, sometimes in poverty and ignominy, now moving up and now moving down. The one thing we can be sure of is that the wheel will revolve. But we must not live on the rim of that wheel, clinging to the shifting, fading, and unreliable goods of the world. Rather we must situate ourselves in the center, at the still-point where Christ stands. From this vantage point, we can watch the wheel turn, finally indifferent to success or failure, long life or short life, adulation or condemnation. At the center of the wheel we assume the attitude of spiritual freedom that the soul masters call "detachment." In a song recorded just weeks before he died, John Lennon sang,

> I'm just sitting here watching the wheels go
>   round and round
> I really love to watch them roll.
> No longer riding on the merry-go-round.

He was celebrating the same liberating detachment symbolized in the wheel of fortune. Oscillating from adulation to obscurity, worrying whether he was moving up or down in popular esteem was, for

Lennon, riding on the merry-go-round, living on the rim of the wheel. Wisdom came when he was detached from his shifting fortune and able to "watch the wheel."

The rose window lures us into this centered place of freedom.

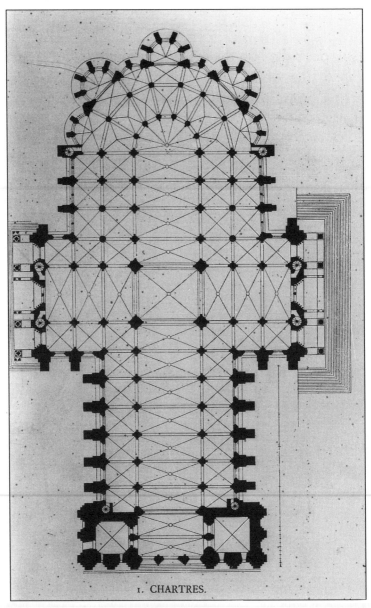

1. CHARTRES.

Ground plan of Chartres Cathedral, France.
(Foto Marburg/Art Resource, NY)

4

Cruciformity

THERE IS AN ASPECT of a cathedral that can easily go undetected if we examine the building only from ground level. However, if we look down at a cathedral from high above (aerial photography is most helpful here), we cannot miss one of its most remarkable characteristics, its cruciformity. The building itself *is* a cross, the main body of the church, the nave, constituting the upright, and the "transept" forming the great crossbeam. When pilgrims visited Notre-Dame de Paris or Chartres or Amiens, they would make their way along the walls of the church, visiting the various shrines and altars. In so doing, whether they knew it or not, they made the way of the cross, since the cross is embedded in the very structure of the place. To the cathedral pilgrim, a confrontation with Jesus' terrible death is inescapable, inevitable.

This is one of the most powerful ways that the cathedrals witness to the nature of Christianity. When St. Paul wanted to communicate to the Corinthians what stood at the very heart of his message he said, "I preach one thing: Christ and him crucified!" In his first evangelical preaching recorded in the Acts of the Apostles, St. Peter sums up his proclamation: "The one you nailed to a cross, God raised up." Indeed one of the distinctive marks of Christianity vis-à-vis other great world religions is the manner of its founder's death. Mohammed dies full of years, honored, and surrounded by friends and family; the Buddha dies peacefully at the end of a long and eventful life, sure that his teaching would be carried on by devoted disciples. But Jesus dies young, alone, abandoned even by his closest friends, by all accounts a failure, hung on a brutal instrument of torture. And this death, the first Christians insisted, was not simply a tragedy, a calamity from which we should turn our eyes, a sad end to a beautiful life; rather, somehow it was the whole point.

Even a cursory reading of the Gospels reveals that Jesus' death is the center and goal of the narrative, that which animates and gives verve to the story. It has often been remarked that the Gospels are not so much biographies of Jesus as "passion narratives with long introductions." Jesus speaks frequently of his "hour," the culmination of his preaching and action, and this hour coincides with his coming to the cross. After his relatively peaceful Galilean ministry, Jesus "sets his face toward Jerusalem," steeling himself for the encounter with the powers of darkness that would take place there and moving with resolution to battle. In the ironic and poetic language of the Gospel of John, the crucified Jesus is "lifted up" in the double sense of suspended above the earth and glorified. And perhaps the most disturbing mystery of the New Testament is that this culminating event of Jesus' life, this macabre glorification through crucifixion, is not simply the result of evil human choices; it is also willed by the one whom Jesus called "Abba, Father." Somehow, it is the deepest purpose of the Incarnation; somehow it is why he was sent.

How can we make sense of this stubborn cruciformity of Christianity, set so permanently in the stone of the cathedrals? We can do so only if we remember that God *is love*.

In our pride, our rebellion, our cruelty, and above all in our fear, we human beings had changed ourselves into a dysfunctional family. Designed to soar into the fullness of God, we had turned ourselves tragically inward, locking ourselves into the cramped and icy space of sin. In order to lure us out of this nightmare, God had sent the prophets and sages of Israel; through them God had crafted covenant after covenant with us, only to see them broken one after another. When all seemed hopeless for us, when it appeared as though the human race was doomed to self-destruction, God, who had spoken in many and varied ways, now spoke to us by his Son. God sent, not simply a prophet, a representative, a plenipotentiary, but his own Self, his own heart. And this divine Son, incarnate in Jesus of Nazareth, entered the darkness and the tempest of human disorder. He went to the poor, the hungry, the self-righteous, those drunk on power and those with no power — to everyone languishing in the iciness of the far country — and he called them home.

Now what is death but the furthest outpost of the far country and the coldest place in the Arctic landscape of sin? Therefore, the assault on death was the ultimate mission of the Son of God. There could be no place untouched by the divine mercy, no refuge from the press of God's relentless love. So God died that we might never be alone and hopeless even in this most desolate of places. When Jesus cries out "My God, my God, why have you abandoned me?" we hear not just the plea of a desperate man; we hear the agonized shout of God himself. Chesterton said it: on the cross God becomes an atheist. God, in Christ, knows what it is like to be left alone, in pain, sinking into the jaws of death, and therefore God becomes our friend, our brother, our fellow-sufferer, even in that most terrible moment.

And this is why St. Paul can exclaim, "I am certain that neither death nor life, neither angels nor principalities, neither height nor depth, nor any other creature can ever separate me from the love of God that comes in Christ Jesus our Lord." Because God has established his power even at the furthest outpost of the far country, there is literally nowhere to hide from him. Because the Son has gone to the limits of godforsakenness, we run from the Father only to find ourselves, at the end of our running, in the arms of the Son. As parents would go anywhere — into prison, to a foreign land, into the gravest danger — to rescue their children, so God, the parent of the human race, went into the darkest reaches of body and soul in order to save us. And therefore this is the meaning of the cross: God is heartbroken love.

There is a terrible interpretation of the cross that has, unfortunately, infected the minds of many Christians. This is the view that the bloody sacrifice of the Son on the cross was "satisfying" to the Father, an appeasement of a God infinitely angry at sinful humanity. In this reading, the crucified Jesus is like a child hurled into the fiery mouth of a pagan divinity in order to assuage its wrath. It is no wonder that many, formed by this cruel theology, find the Christian doctrine of the cross hard to accept: I once heard the objection that this sacrifice of the Son to the Father constitutes an act of cosmic child abuse.

What eloquently gives the lie to this awful interpretation is the passage from John's Gospel that is

often proposed as a summary of the Christian message: "God so loved the world, that he sent his only
Son, that all who believe in him might have life in his
name." It is not out of anger or vengeance or in a desire for retribution that the Father sends the Son but
precisely out of love. God the Father is not some pa-
thetic divinity whose bruised personal honor needs
to be restored; rather God is a parent who burns
with compassion for his children who have wandered
into danger. Does the Father hate sinners? No, but
he hates sin. Does God harbor indignation at the unjust? No, but God despises injustice. Thus God sends
his Son, not gleefully to see him suffer, but to set
things right.

St. Anselm, the great medieval theologian, who is
often unfairly blamed for the cruel theology of satis-
faction, was eminently clear on this score. We sinners
are like diamonds that have fallen into the muck;
made in the image of God, we have soiled ourselves
through violence and hatred. God, claimed Anselm,
could have simply pronounced a word of forgiveness from heaven; but this would not have solved the
problem. It would not have restored the diamonds
to their original brilliance. Instead, in his passion to
reestablish the beauty of creation, God came down
into the muck of sin and death and brought the diamonds up and polished them off. In so doing of
course, God had to get dirty. This sinking into the

dirt — this divine solidarity with the lost — is the "sacrifice" which the Son makes to the infinite plea-sure of the Father. It is a sacrifice expressive, not of anger or vengeance, but of compassion.

Jesus said that any disciple of his must be willing to take up his cross and follow the master. If God is self-forgetting love even to the point of death, then we must be such love. If God is willing to break open his own heart, then we must be willing to break open our hearts for others. The cross, in short, must be-come the very structure of the Christian life. And this is why medieval Christians worked the cross into the structures of their most sacred buildings. They de-termined that when we gaze at the splendor of the cathedral — at the ordered beauty of its façade, at the finery of its ornamentation, at the graceful rhythm of its composition, at the elegance of its spires — we are gazing, inescapably, at the cross. And they de-termined that as we walk through it, admiring its variegated faces and aspects, we are, unavoidably, walking through the cross.

The cruciform cathedrals teach us that we must never forget what God has done on our behalf, and we must never fail to make that love the structure and foundation of our lives.

The heavens declare the glory of God (Psalm 18:2)
Figures from the central west portal, Chartres Cathedral, France.
(The Crosiers – Gene Plaisted, OSC)

5

Cosmic Consciousness

IT SEEMS AS THOUGH a major concern of eccle-
sial architects today is to make us feel at home.
Churches have come to resemble living rooms, or
shopping malls, and even our manner of describing
them is comforting and domestic: they are "gathering
spaces" or "worship centers." But when we enter a
Gothic cathedral we feel anything but "at home"; it
seems, on the contrary, that we are entering another
world — or better, worlds.

In Dante's *Divine Comedy,* Satan is depicted as
buried up to his waist in ice at the bottom of Hell.
His kingdom — that area over which he has imme-
diate control — extends just as far as the limits of
his own body. Though he flaps his massive wings
day and night, he goes nowhere and succeeds only
in making the world around him colder. This fallen
and immobile angel beautifully evokes St. Augustine's definition of sin as *curvatus in se,* being turned
in on oneself. Sinners are those who make themselves undisputed lord and master of a very tiny

realm: the kingdom of the ego. When Dante finishes his journey through Hell and Purgatory and arrives in Heaven, he begins effortlessly to fly, walking the sky from planet to planet. This nimbleness and subtlety of movement is meant to contrast sharply with Satan's icy immobility. To be in sin is to live in one very small space, whereas to be in God's grace is to course with abandon through myriad worlds, moving ever upward and onward. "Why can the angels fly?" Chesterton asks. "Because they take themselves so lightly." The Gothic cathedrals are designed to facilitate flight — away from the tiny, cramped room of the ego.

The first world into which the cathedrals invite us is that of the earth. Medieval people loved the earth — and all that grows from it or moves upon it — for they saw it with biblical eyes: God made the sea, the dry land, the plants and animals and insects, pronouncing all of them good. Therefore, God's house ought to teem with life. Accordingly, everywhere you turn in a Gothic cathedral, you see, carved in the stones and etched in the glass, God's exuberant creation: vines, leaves, tendrils, trees, birds, fish, sheep, and dogs. The nave of Notre-Dame de Paris is lined with stately Corinthian columns each topped with an elaborate leafy design. These pillars were intended to suggest a forest of trees, calling to mind the garden of paradise from which we fell and

for which we long. And high up in the towers of
the Laon cathedral — in the place where one might
expect to find angels — are sixteen carved oxen, a
tribute to the beasts of burden who carried the stones
to the building site.

This raising up of particularly humble, inelegant
animals to the highest place in the cathedral obvi-
ously struck the medieval mind as not the least bit
odd. The delicacy with which these things of nature
are depicted reveals unmistakably the attentiveness
and affection of the artists. Some of the founders of
"creation spirituality" in our time have legitimately
traced the lineage of their teaching back to the mystics and theologians of the Middle Ages. There are
indeed no greater shrines to a spirituality of the
earth than the Gothic cathedrals produced by the
medieval mind.

Yet, the decentering of the ego does not stop here,
for there are other worlds into which the cathedrals
want to lure us. All over these great churches, we can
find evocations of the cosmos: planets, stars, the open
sky; in fact the dramatic verticality of the buildings
compel the gaze of the spirit upward. On the very
summit of the twin towers of Chartres, for example,
we can see images of the sun and the moon, and
on the façade of Notre-Dame de Paris there is an
elaborate depiction of the signs of the zodiac.

According to the medieval scientists and philoso-

phers, the earth is surrounded by translucent spheres
on which the moon and the various planets are fixed.
As these spheres turn, they produce an inaudible
harmony (the music of the spheres) that provides
the foundation for all earthly music and even for
the harmonies and relationships explored by math-
ematicians. And as biblically formed people, these
cosmologists knew that "the heavens proclaim the
glory of God and the firmament shows forth his
majesty." They believed, in short, that God offered to
them in the heavens a sort of archetype or exemplar
the imitation of which would perfect minds, hearts,
and societies here below. So, after looking carefully
around them to the things of the earth, they looked
up, rather intently, and brought what they saw into
their sacred buildings.

However, the flight of the spirit continues. Beyond
the earth and beyond even the heavenly spheres lies a
properly supernatural dimension of God's creation,
the realm of the angels and saints. It is central to
a Christian consciousness that the holy ones who
have passed away are not dead, but are rather even
more vibrantly alive. As we saw, the churches dedicated to Notre-Dame are not simply monuments
to Mary; they are her earthly dwelling place. She
is stubbornly *there*. And so the blessed dead — pa-
triarchs, prophets, soldiers, mystics, preachers, and
apostles — surround the visitor to a Gothic cathe-

dral. They frame the doorways, hover in the stained glass, preside in the spires and towers; and, in some cases, their bodies lie under the floors and their relics in the altars. Their world and ours — though separated by a great ontological gulf — nevertheless interpenetrate, prayer and loving concern moving in both directions and the cathedral functioning as a sort of medium of exchange.

Then there are the angels who swarm and swoop over the cathedrals. Around the tympanum over the main portal of Notre-Dame de Paris is depicted a whole crowd of them witnessing the drama of the Last Judgment. Some rest their heads pensively on their hands; some lean over the railing for a better view, like theater-goers; some giggle and grin, others pull sad faces; some fold their hands in pious prayer. Decorating the façade of Reims Cathedral are sculptures that are among the most mysterious and beautiful works of medieval art: angels with alluring and slightly unsettling smiles. On the furthest point of Chartres, on the roof just over the apse, there stands an angel who can be rotated to face the four points of the compass: he represents the proclamation of the Gospel to the ends of the earth.

Thomas Aquinas taught that angels are pure spirits, intelligences totally separate from matter, beings capable of godlike speed and precision in their reasoning and perception. Standing close to the Fire, they share more intensely in the pitch and perfection of the divine being; indeed the highest angels are called seraphim precisely because they are burnt and scorched by the presence of God.

The wonderfully good news announced by the cathedrals is that these sublime creatures *have to do with us*. They involve themselves in the history of our salvation, acting as messengers, conduits, companions, and they thereby link us to reaches of God's creation that go beyond what we can see, imagine, or measure. Hamlet said to his friend Horatio, "There are more things in heaven and on earth than are dreamed of in your philosophies." Shakespeare's hero was challenging his interlocutor's cramped rationalism that could not push beyond the relatively superficial realm of what can be controlled and ordered by the mind. So the angels of the cathedrals compel our spirits (crippled by the cold empiricism of the Enlightenment) out past the world of nature, past the cosmos itself, into the forecourts of God's house.

Perhaps the most important thing that the cosmic cathedrals help us to realize is that these various worlds are *connected*. The earth (and all of its denizens), the heavens, the planets and stars, the blessed dead, the angels and archangels — all are creatures of the one God; all pour forth continually from the same divine source. And therefore all are brothers and sisters to one another, linked at the center. One of the greatest spirits of the Middle Ages, Francis of Assisi, said precisely this in his cosmic hymn, the Canticle of the Sun, his language both poetic and metaphysically exact: "brother sun and sister moon; brother fire and sister water." The universe is composed, not of atomistic individuals, but of interdependent organs in a body. The cathedrals speak the truth that the entirety of the cosmos, from the seraphim to the simplest elements, form that perfect and complex body which is "Christ come to full stature."

The Last Judgment, tympanum of central portal. Notre-Dame, Paris, France. (Alinari/Art Resource, NY)

6

The Last Judgment

W HAT WE SPONTANEOUSLY call the front of a cathedral — the façade and towers — is in fact the back. Almost all the Gothic cathedrals are oriented, that is to say, they face the rising sun, and the eastern point of these churches is not the façade but the apse. When the medieval priest celebrated Mass, he was situated in the apsidal end of the cathedral and he looked to the east — away from the people and the main portals. This orientation was of great spiritual moment, for all of Christian life is a looking to the one who called himself the light of the world and a longing for the one who is the rising Son of God.

But when we turn toward something, we inevitably turn away from something else; to set our face is also to set our back. Therefore, the backside of the cathedral symbolizes the Christian resistance to all that is opposed to the light of Christ. If the apse faces the rising sun, the façade confronts the setting sun and all the powers of darkness. It is the church's great "no" to violence, self-absorption, and hatred — all the works of the Devil. And this of course is why there is a fierce, bristling, looming quality to so many of the Gothic fronts: they are the fighting face of Christianity.

But do we Christians fight with our own weapons and according to our own powers? Of course not! Indeed, when we have tried over the centuries to do just that, we have succeeded only in making matters worse. What we must fight with are the spiritual weapons that Paul named: the helmet of righteousness and the breastplate of salvation and the sword of justice, in other words, with the power of Christ's incarnation.

According to the early Church Fathers, Christ's coming precipitated a warfare with the powers that hold the world in their sway. In bringing God's *ordo,* God's arrangement, to the world, Jesus had to move into the arena of disorder, but this invasion was not met with passivity or acquiescence. Rather, the principalities of the world — Herod, Pilate, the scribes and Pharisees, the demons — waged a ferocious struggle against him, and it was only through the drama of the cross and resurrection that Jesus managed to defeat them. He took all of their violence and through courageous forgiveness robbed it of its authority, for violence feeds on itself, surviving only through reproduction. When it is met with

compassion and forgiveness, it dissipates, its power-source gone. In the language of the Fathers, Jesus thereby tied up the Devil, frustrating him into submission, leading our captivity to hatred captive. So as the hymn text has it: "the strife is o'er the battle done; ... the victory won." Karl Barth said that the principal task of the Christian preacher is to proclaim to the battle-weary world that the war is over.

Now when Christians announce that the battle is over, they do not ignore the fact that there is plenty of evil left to fight. They proclaim that the decisive battle has been won and that the enemy has, in principle, been defeated, even though pockets of resistance remain. And, as any soldier who fought in the Battle of the Bulge can testify, the struggles after the climactic conflict are sometimes the most ferocious and brutal, since the enemy knows that time is short. So in the spiritual realm: though Christ has defeated the enemy, we must still join him in the dangerous and exhilarating closing battles, and we must

use the weapons that he used. We must, like the cathedral façade, stand against the works of the Devil,
putting on the armor of Christ.

It is here that the façade of Notre-Dame de Paris
is particularly evocative. If we examine the lines and
rhythms of the cathedral front with special attention, we see that everything is just a bit off. There
is a triangular design over the left portal but not
over the right; the openings in the bell towers are
of slightly different widths; the number of kings on
the left side is eight while the number on the right is
seven — and many more of these discrepancies could
be noted. Do we conclude that the architects were
imprecise in their measurements? Hardly likely in a
culture where number, balance and symmetry were
everywhere reverenced.

What the architects wanted in fact to communicate
was the imperfection and sinfulness of the universe, a
lack of proportion that often effectively masks itself
behind the veneer of beauty. Now in the very heart
of this flawed design is the flawless circle, which is
the west rose window. For the medieval world, the
circle is the perfect shape, having no beginning or end
and subsisting in a splendid geometrical harmony.
The spiritual lesson is clear: into our imperfect and
disharmonious world has come the perfection of the
Son of God, the divine entering into flesh in order
to save it and reorder it. The circle in the off-kilter

square is therefore a lovely symbol of the Incarnation. This is the façade which rears up against the realm of the setting sun; this is the shield that the church holds up against the forces of violence; this is the message shouted to the dark world.

Over the main portal at Notre-Dame (and at almost all the other cathedrals) is a depiction of the Last Judgment, the event that will take place when the sun sets on time itself. Jesus stands majestically in the middle, surveying the scene, while at his feet is the archangel Michael weighing in his scales the souls of the dead. Those who are found wanting are led off by demons to damnation, and those who are worthy are led to paradise. The biblical warrant for this awful picture is, of course, the twenty-fifth chapter of Matthew's Gospel: "All the nations will be gathered before him, and he will separate people one from another as a shepherd separates the sheep from the goats."

The idea of Jesus as judge is one with which we are distinctly uncomfortable; yet even the most cursory reading of the New Testament reveals how unavoidable this is. Christ can be gentle (as when he invited the children to come to him), *and* he can be ferocious (as when he hurled invective at the Pharisees or turned over the money-changers' tables). Indeed Chesterton said that in front of every church there ought to be a statue of the compassionate Jesus *and* a statue of Christ in full flight of fury, since both are indisputably present in the Gospel stories. The point is that when God's own *ordo* appears in the world, he, necessarily, judges the disorder that surrounds him.

To judge, in the biblical sense of the term, means to bring into the light, to throw into sharp relief. When good and evil are confused or intermingled, divine judgment separates them, clarifying the issue. By his very nature, in his every word and gesture, in the very way that he stood, Jesus, God's Word, was a judge. He was the light of the world, harshly exposing that which would prefer to remain in the dark; he was the unadulterated criterion, the truth in the presence of which falsity necessarily appeared for what it was.

Bob Dylan said, "The enemy I see wears the cloak of decency." One of the favorite ruses of evil is to cover itself in the mantle of justice and piety, at the same time aping and hiding behind that which it opposes. The first demon that Jesus confronts in Mark's Gospel is in a synagogue, because a house of God is often the preferred lair of the evil one, and Jesus' greatest enemies are those swathed in the most impressive religious titles and garments. Christ's judgment rips away these cloaking devices, these deceits, and shows things as they are. In Flannery O'Connor's "A Good Man Is Hard to Find," the

Misfit, a ruthless killer, displays a surprisingly accurate grasp of Christology. When the name of Jesus is mentioned, he says, "Ah yes, Jesus, he throwed everything off." We live in a kinky, off-kilter world, a place where, again to quote Bob Dylan, "you find out when you reach the top, you're on the bottom." It is this off-centered moral universe that Jesus "throws off," thereby tipping it back into balance.

Authentic Christianity is a fighting religion, and it calls evil by its name. There is a legitimate inclusivity to the religion of Christ, since it seeks to draw the whole world into the embrace of love; but there is a hard-edged and uncompromising exclusivity to it as well. The church knows what stands outside of itself, and it turns its back on it. The bearer of light and truth, it separates good from evil, sometimes painfully, "like a two-edged sword." The dark, brooding faces of the cathedrals testify to it: "the one who does not gather with me scatters."

Sculptures from the central north portal, Chartres Cathedral, France —
from left: Melchisedek, Abraham and Isaac, Moses, Samuel,
King David. (Foto Marburg/Art Resource, NY)

7

Our Jewish Origins

Like Christianity itself, the cathedrals are inescapably Jewish. When I was a student in France, I spent an entire weekend at Chartres Cathedral, climbing the towers, examining each of the windows, and painstakingly inspecting each of the sculptures that surround the portals. Though there were plenty of scenes and images evocative of the New Testament, what specially struck me was how thoroughly the building engaged my Old Testament imagination. Job, Aaron, Adam, Moses, Isaiah, Jeremiah, Jesse, David, and Saul are just a few of the Old Testament figures that adorn the cathedral. Though it is all about Christ and his paschal mystery, Chartres Cathedral will not allow the viewer to separate Christ from the strange, loamy, densely textured world out of which he arose and in which alone he becomes intelligible. It states concretely what Pope Pius XI said in the 1930s: "We Christians are all spiritually Semites."

In the second century, there emerged the Marcionite heresy, named for its propagator, Marcion. According to this view — prevalent at various times in the history of the church and present even today — the true revelation of God that occurred in Jesus effectively supersedes the revelation of the Old Testament, turning it finally into something false and misleading. On this Marcionite reading, the spiritual God of tender compassion disclosed by Christ has nothing to do with the crude and jealous creator God of the Hebrew Scriptures. Marcion himself accepted only the letters of Paul — with their strong polemic against the law — and the Gospel of Luke, seeing everything else in the Bible as tainted by the Jewish contagion. One of the most important decisions made by the early church was to resist the Marcionite temptation and to affirm the integrity of revelation: the God who speaks definitively in Christ is the same God who spoke in the prophecies, persons and dramas of the Hebrew Scriptures. In a word, creation and redemption come from the same source.

So how did the early theologians read the relationship between the two testaments? If we turn to the biblical commentaries and sermons of Augustine, Chrysostom, Gregory of Nyssa, and especially Origen of Alexandria, we have our answer: the Old Testament is a symbolic anticipation of the New, the hidden and figurative hint at what becomes manifest in Christ. Thus, there is a curious and mutually illumining mirroring that takes place between the testaments, each story, personage, and event of the one finding its counterpart in the other.

The Church Fathers certainly read the Hebrew Scriptures through the lens of the Gospels, but it is equally valid to say that their interpretive instinct was to move in the opposite direction as well. When we see two photographs of the same man, one taken when he was a child and the other as an adult, an intriguing tension is set up between the pictures. Now we see the child in light of the man he would become, and we perceive the man as the development of the child he once was, each photo living in the interpretive aura of the other. There is something very similar regarding the overlapping of the Christ-in-shadows of the Hebrew Scriptures and the Christ-in-light of the New Testament.

This patristic vision is incarnated no more dramatically than on the north porch of Chartres Cathedral, where a series of beautifully preserved statues of Old Testament figures is arranged on either side of the portal. They are on the north side of the building because that is the side that receives less light in the course of the day, and they are the shadowy anticipations of the light of Christ. We see Melchisedek, the priest of Salem, holding the sacrificial bread and wine which foreshadow the bread and wine transformed by Christ at the Last Supper. Next to him is Abraham, one hand under the chin of his son Isaac and the other gripping the knife of slaughter, anticipating the terrible drama in which God the Father sacrifices his beloved Son on the cross. Then we find Moses holding up the bronze serpent, which healed the people in the desert. This hints at Christ, raised up on the cross in order to effect the salvation (the healing) of the world. To Moses' left is the prophet Samuel putting a knife to the throat of a lamb, thereby foreshadowing the sacrifice of the one who is called the Lamb of God. And finally we see King David, the author of Psalm 22, which describes the passion of the one who was hailed as the son of David and who died under the ironic sign "King of the Jews." Lest we miss the connection, David holds the crown of thorns and the lance that pierced the side of Jesus.

What I find particularly arresting about these figures is the dignity and serene beauty of their postures and facial expressions. They are not only serious (*gravitas* is a virtue that even the ancient Romans admired); they are peaceful, at rest, centered, and sure of themselves, as though they have found their place. And that is just the point. Arranged around the portal of Christ's house, they have found their raison d'être, the deepest purpose of their life-dramas, the accomplishment of their missions. The Hebrew Scriptures rest and nest in the horizon of meaning opened up by the Christ of the New Testament.

Another rich example of the intertwining of the testaments can be found inside Chartres on the colored window telling the twin stories of the Fall and Redemption and the Good Samaritan. By weaving the two accounts together, the artist compels us to read them in unison. Through sin, we human beings fell from grace and lost our likeness to God, becom-ing like the man in Jesus' parable who fell in with robbers on the road to Jericho and was left beaten and half-dead by the side of the road. The law, the temple, the theocratic institutions of Israel could not save us, just as the priest and the Levite fail the wounded man in Jesus' story. Finally there came to us a stranger, sharing our nature but also transcending it, one of us but also the totally Other, who had compassion on us in our helplessness and deigned to carry our burden for us and to pay our debt of sin. So the Good Samaritan — a half-breed, familiar and strange — had compassion on the dying man and lifted him on his beast of burden, carrying him to an inn, nursing him, and promising to pay for him. This bold and unabashed juxtaposition of Old Testament and New, of parable and doctrine, of Christ and Adam is characteristically medieval. Since the entire Bible flows ultimately from the same source, every word throws light on every other word.

Now there is, admittedly, a dark side to all of this. Even while they celebrate the Jewish prefiguring of Christ, the cathedrals express a disdain for the Jews who did not accept the Messiah. On numerous windows in the Gothic cathedrals, Jews are depicted with stereotypically ugly features and portrayed as villains in the stories of the saints. They are associated with the Devil, seen as the descendants of the Pharisees, and placed on the left side of the cross along with the disbelieving "bad thief." Perhaps the most common anti-Semitic image from the cathedrals is that of the blindfolded woman, a deposed queen with her crown on the ground. Overthrown, stripped of power, and unable to see spiritually, she stands for the synagogue, once the gathering place of God's chosen people but now a center of disbelief and sin. She is often coupled with a contrasting image of the church, a jauntily posed woman, wearing her crown and gazing confidently forward.

One could argue that this negative attitude toward unbelieving Jews has its roots in the New Testament itself (indeed the trope of the unseeing synagogue is from the letters of Paul) and thus is a legitimate expression of Christian faith. But this reading becomes intellectually untenable when we examine the New Testament in its entirety, bearing in mind especially that Paul himself took the reconciliation between Christians and the children of Israel to be of tremendous spiritual importance. And it becomes morally untenable when we remember that there were communities of Jews in the cathedral towns of Europe, people who suffered on a daily basis the dire consequences of the anti-Semitic attitudes embedded in the artwork of these houses of God.

We can only conclude that the Jewish aspect of the cathedrals is in part their glory and in part their shame.

The crypt door. Chartres Cathedral, France.
(Foto Marburg /Art Resource, NY)

8

The Crypt

W HEN MEDIEVAL PILGRIMS came to Chartres, they
certainly studied the statues and marveled at the
windows that adorned the upper church, but their
main purpose was to go underground, to the crypt
underneath the cathedral, there to pray before the
statue of the Black Virgin. This was a small sculpture in wood of a mother and child said to date from
the primeval period when Druid priests performed
their sacred rites in the region of Chartres. In fact
the claim was made that even the Druids, mysteri-
ously anticipating Christianity, honored this woman
as a virgin mother. In the dank and somber space of
the crypt, the medieval pilgrim communed with this
swarthy statue, leaving behind the luminous glories
of the cathedral above. Oddly, this was the point, the
final destination of the pilgrimage.

Christians have always felt an attraction for these
dark and chthonic places: whether it was the early
believers hiding in the catacombs of Rome or the
saints Jerome, Antony, Benedict, and Ignatius of Loy-

ola fleeing to caves in order to pray, or visitors to
Lourdes swarming into a massive underground basilica. Perhaps the attraction is rooted in Christmas, the
day when the Son of God was born, as Chesterton
put it, in a cave under the earth; or maybe it comes
from Good Friday, the day when Christ was placed in
a tomb hewn from the rock. Whatever the source, it
remains true that when Christians venture into these
sacred underground places, they feel, not threatened
or claustrophobic, but at home, almost as though
they are in the embrace of a mother.

In the biblical and theological tradition of Christianity, there are ample references to the transcendence and otherness of God. Thus Isaiah insists that
God is as high above us as the heavens are above
the earth; Moses tells us that God's real name cannot be pronounced; Thomas Aquinas never tires of
reminding us that the essence of the divine remains
incomprehensible, and Karl Barth defended throughout his career what he called the "godliness of God"
against all attempts to domesticate the sacred. But
this is only part of the story. Were God nothing but
transcendent, he would devolve into a distant philosophical principle or, even worse, into a capricious
tyrant, like so many of the gods of Greek mythology.

Accordingly, the great tradition puts a balancing
stress on the divine immanence: with Augustine it
says that God is "closer than we are to ourselves,"

and with Aquinas it holds that God is in all things "most intimately," and with Paul Tillich it asserts that God is the "ground of our being." What I have always loved about Tillich's description is how it highlights the humility (literally close to the *humus* or the ground) and indirection of God. The divine power is not that which immediately draws attention to itself, but rather that which is under or behind all things, like a mother who effaces herself that her children might shine.

The ground of being is thoroughly and inescapably at work in all of creation, though always clandestinely so. There is something dark and close, intimate and deeply reassuring about the way God acts, so that we can say with Isaiah: "as a child rests in his mother's arms even so my soul." To be sure, God must be high enough not to be manipulated, but God also must be low enough not to be avoided. If God is like a father, the Lord of the heavens, God is also like a mother, a nurturing and sustaining source. I wonder whether it was this cozy intimacy with the holy that the pilgrims sought when they plunged underground to pray before the Black Virgin.

But this earthiness of God has another dimension as well. The *humus,* the earth, the cave — all of these are also frightening places. They teem with the lower animals — insects, rats, bats, and vermin — and they are, traditionally, the dwelling places of preternatural beings — spirits, sprites, goblins, and vampires. In the mythologies and folktales of primal peoples, one courts danger when one burrows into the ground or explores the labyrinthine ways of a cavern. In light of the Incarnation, Christians can say that God has gone to these dangerous places and sanctified them, that God has visited these frightening corners and illumined them.

Paul tells us that "though Christ was in the form of God, he did not deem equality with God a thing to be grasped at" and instead emptied himself and became a creature, a denizen of the earth. In Jesus, the Son of God pushed his way into finitude, into flesh, into bones and blood, into the dirt, and what he thereby effected was a remaking of the whole of material creation. For nothing in the world stands in ontological independence; no man (indeed no thing) is an island, but rather all created beings are interwoven, implicated in one another. Every action of yours sets off a reaction in the world around you the contours of which you can barely begin to imagine. How much more dramatically therefore does the enfleshment of the Word of God affect the material cosmos. Christ's coming is like the detonation of an underground nuclear device which sends shock waves throughout the surrounding territory; or it is like a waterfall that crashes into a lake, churning it and kicking up mud from the bottom.

Thus, Jesus transforms all of matter. He divinizes the highest and the lowest, the brightest and the most obscure. Therefore, in even the most frightening places — even the *humus* of the tomb itself — we can feel, oddly enough, at home. This is why, for example, in the deeply Christian telling of the vampire legend, Bram Stoker's *Dracula,* the adventurers can confront the darkest power provided they are armed with the cross. It is God's journey into the lowest place — symbolized by the crucifix — that has rendered powerless all those things that have terrified and preyed upon the human race: they are driven out by God's entering in.

And there is something else about crypts, caves, and caverns. They speak of that deep, dark, and permanent religiosity that unites the race, that *philosophia perennis* that can be discerned in the rituals, speculations, and mystical strivings of the wisdom figures of the world. One of the precious characteristics of Catholic Christianity is that, in the words of Ewert Cousins, "it never threw anything away." Catholicism recognized Christ as the fullness of revelation — God's own Word become manifest — but in so doing, at its best, it did not despise the innumerable ways in which that Word is partially, yet truly, revealed. Thus it demonstrated what Cardinal Newman called "the power of assimilation," the generous willingness to draw into its fullness all that is true and good in the religions and philosophies that it encountered.

The organizational structure of the Roman empire, the ceremonial of the Byzantine court, the philosophies of Aristotle and Plotinus and Kant, the metaphysics and architecture of the Islamic world, the prayer forms of Judaism, the mysticism of the Celts, and, yes, even the processions of the Druids — all of these expressions of the divine Logos were included in the *communio* of the church of Jesus Christ. Authentic Catholicism never defended the finally impossible thesis that its religion is simply right and all the others simply wrong, for it sensed that such a view would denigrate the very creative Logos that came to us in Jesus. What it did claim is that all of these spiritualities find their home in the church, discovering in the light of Christ their own deepest identity and purpose.

This is what we see in the cathedral of Chartres resting on and towering above its crypt. In one sense, the church of Christ *stands on* the great religious feeling of the human race; it is immersed in that deep river that constitutes religiosity itself. But then it rises above that foundation, and it surges up out of that river, revealing itself as something new and fresh and unheard of. The Fourth Lateran Council formulated a principle that applies here: *in tantu similitudine maior dissimilitudo* (in however great a similarity an even greater dissimilarity). There is indeed a continuity between the religions of the world and the church of Jesus, but even in that similarity there is a greater dissimilarity, and, in the final analysis, the latter is more striking than the former.

Perhaps at the end of this meditation, I can effect a reversal. I began by saying that the pilgrim came to the crypt as to a final destination, and this remains, in one sense, true. But something tells me that after bathing in the sweet darkness of the underground chapel, that pilgrim would be compelled by the dynamism of his Christian spirit to come up out of the earth — to the air, to the color, to the light.

Notre-Dame Cathedral, Amiens, France. Interior view of nave
toward east. (Foto Marburg/Art Resource, NY)

9

Verticality

WHEN WE FIRST ENTER a Gothic cathedral, we are, as we saw earlier, blinded, plunged into darkness. However, once our eyes adjust and the interior becomes visible, our heads are wrenched almost automatically up, because every major line in the building is vertical, shooting skyward like an arrow. I have seen it numerous times: groups of people making their way through the nave of a major cathedral and moving, not with confidence and purpose, but slowly, meditatively, drifting like a school of lazy fish, their eyes trained on the distant heights of the structure. The building forces the visitors out of themselves, inviting them to transcendence.

We spoke earlier of certain innovations in engineering (including flying buttresses) that made this soaring verticality possible, and it is safe to say that Gothic architects reveled in it, each one trying to outstrip the other, much like the designers of skyscrapers today. So St. Denis is topped by Notre-Dame de Paris, which is outstripped by Chartres, which is surpassed by the cathedral of Cologne, and all of them are dwarfed by the cathedral of Beauvais, which grew so high that it eventually collapsed, putting some medieval thinkers in mind of the Tower of Babel. We can only imagine the impact that these buildings had on the people of the Middle Ages when even today, in the age of skyscrapers, they seem dizzyingly tall.

As we have come to expect, this architectural feature was designed, not simply to impress, but to teach and inspire. Something that is rooted deep in the biblical tradition and that distinguished the faith of the Jews from the religions and mythologies that surrounded them, is the conviction that God is not the world. Many spiritual systems — from nature mysticism to Greek mythology to Gnosticism to the contemporary New Age movement — concur in holding that the divine is an immanent power in or of the world. When the Jewish scripture announces "in the beginning, God created the heavens and the earth," it signals a radical difference in spiritual perception. All things above and below are related to God, *but they are not God;* all that is true and beautiful in the finite realm is a reflection of God, *but it is not God.*

In a famous meditation in the tenth book of his *Confessions,* St. Augustine interrogates the elements of nature wondering whether they might be divine: "the sea and the deeps . . . the things that creep . . . the winds that blow...the heavens, the sun, the moon and the stars" join in unison and deny their divinity, saying, "We are not the God whom you seek; look higher." When the best and brightest citizens of the cosmos can say together "look higher," we have pushed beyond all forms of immanent mysticism to a spirituality of creation, that is to say, of separation and divine transcendence.

The staggering verticality of the cathedrals is in service of this mysticism of otherness. These sacred buildings illustrate the Christian belief that God is always "somehow else," beyond what we can experience or speak or conceptualize, beyond the reach of consciousness, will, or imagination, in that trackless realm that is not of this world or of any possible world. Augustine reminded his readers *si comprehendis non est Deus* (if you understand, it is not God), and Aquinas insisted that we never know what God is, only what God is not, and Karl Rahner said that to know God most fully is to know God's incomprehensibility. As they draw us upward, the cathedrals seem to say "not here, not there," and it is thus that they invite us to the silence beyond any speech.

To the otherness and incomprehensibility of God corresponds an appropriate attitude of the spirit that might be termed "restlessness" or "holy longing" or even, to use the words of St. Paul, "groaning." Since

God is unavoidably "somehow else," and since our happiness lies only in God, then we must be uneasy pilgrims in this world. Nothing here below — wealth, success, power, beautiful things, status — can ever satisfy our most pressing desire, and hence we remain constitutionally, permanently on the way somewhere else. We live on earth as resident aliens, since we know that our true citizenship is in the far country of God's mystery.

From this resident alien status there flows, it is true, a permanent unease, but from it also comes a clarity of vision. Because we know that nothing finite is ever our final good, we are not seduced by the inflated claims of the politicians, social theorists, philosophers, and bureaucrats who promise a paradise that will come if only we change this system or modify that economy or rearrange that society. Because our eyes are fixed on the City above, we, paradoxically, see the city below with greater precision and judge it more critically. And this is why the dizzying verticality of the cathedrals is not simply an invitation to contemplate another world (it is indeed that), but is also a reminder to gaze with a cold analytical eye on this world.

Many social commentators in the period just after the Enlightenment condemned the religious attitude as a dangerous block to progress and the fomenter of conflict and violence. If only we moved past the

obsession with another
dimension, they implied,
we would focus our en-
ergies of mind and will
constructively on this one,
and an age of progress
and peace would result.
If the century just end-
ing has proven anything,
it is that these would-
be prophets had it just
about completely back-
ward. The fomenters of

violence on a scale never before seen in history were
not those who looked to God but precisely those who
explicitly denied the spiritual. The ones who forgot
about heaven were those who laid waste the earth.

In the biblical story of Adam and Eve, the basic
psychological and spiritual dynamics of human life
are made plain. The first humans are made in the
image of God and are then placed in a sumptuous
garden where they are given free rein to enjoy all the
fruits and trees that surround them, save only the tree
of the knowledge of good and evil. What is implied
in their ranginess and freedom is God's desire that
human creatures be fully alive, using their powers of
body, imagination, mind, and feeling to the utmost.
To be at play in the garden of the Lord is to cultivate

the sciences and arts, to engage in lively conversation, to cultivate friendship, to explore, claim, and know the world. The lie believed by many throughout the centuries — and embedded in numerous primal myths — is that God is jealous of humans and wants to keep them in their place, hemmed in by oppressive and arbitrary laws. In the vision of Genesis nothing could be further from the truth.

But how then do we interpret the prohibition? If God is not suspicious of them, as the serpent suggests, why does God forbid them from eating of the tree of good and evil? To answer these questions is to come to the heart of the matter. God does indeed want his human creatures to be fully alive, but God knows that this fullness, the pitch of joy, comes when, at the end of all of striving, we allow ourselves to be drawn, when, after a lifetime of seeking, we permit ourselves to be found. There is a rhythm in the good life, an oscillating between grasping and being grasped, achieving and being achieved, breathing in and breathing out. We stand confidently in our accomplishments, and then we must be willing to stand outside of ourselves (*ex-stasis*), as a higher power draws us beyond what we can do. And it is this passivity, this ecstasy, that is far greater than any activity of ours. There is something wonderful as a man and a woman come to know one another, gradually understanding one another's minds and motivations, over time exploring the secrets of each other's personality, but the relationship comes alive only when the two people *fall in love,* when they surrender to something beyond their grasping and controlling.

God prohibits the eating from the tree of the knowledge of good and evil because God wants us to fall in love with him. To eat of the tree is to grasp at a godliness that is attainable only through surrender.

At the heart of Ignatian spirituality is the conviction that God is *semper maior,* always greater. This means, on the theological plain, that no concept or image can ever adequately represent the Lord, but on the spiritual plain it means that we must always be willing to fall more deeply in love with God. As the arches, lines, and towers of the cathedral pull the eye upward, they are also pulling the soul up beyond itself to the far country attainable only through ecstasy.

Notre-Dame, Paris, France. Detail of gargoyle on the balustrade.
(Alinari/Art Resource, NY)

10

Gargoyles

SHAKESPEARE'S GREATEST TRAGEDIES — *Hamlet, Macbeth, Romeo and Juliet* — are interrupted occasionally by scenes of comic relief. The playwright seemed to sense that his audience could not withstand the unrelenting pressure of the drama and had to let off steam, adjusting psychologically before the next act. In a similar way, the *Divine Comedy* of Dante — that intensely theological drama of sin and salvation — is punctuated here and there by grotesqueries, silly conversations, and ludicrous figures. And it is said that at the height of the initiation into the Eleusinian mysteries, that most mystical and profound expression of ancient Greek religion, a comic figure — perhaps a man dressed up as a woman — suddenly appeared in order to provoke laughter among the initiates. Somehow we have always grasped that the most sacred and serious things not only can be but must be accompanied by the ridiculous, lest their *gravitas* devolve into a ponderousness that is just too hard to bear.

We can discern this principle in the odd, comic, bizarre, and just slightly inappropriate figures that pose, prance, dart about, and preen all over the great cathedrals. I am speaking, of course, of the gargoyles and demons. On the towers at Notre-Dame de Paris there sit horned and winged creatures who seem to be scanning the cityscape for prey. And from the edge of the roof jut menacing serpent-like beasts who appear ready at any moment to pounce on some unfortunate passerby. (They also serve a practical function: during rainstorms, water gushes from their mouths onto the street below.) Some gargoyles are monstrous, with ugly facial features and deformed bodies, and others are alarming hybrids of natural forms: a bird's head on a goat's body or a human torso narrowing into the tail of a fish.

One of my favorite grotesques is on the right side of the tympanum above the main portal at Notre-Dame de Paris. She is a female devil with ape-like ears, an impossibly wide mouth from which an insolent tongue protrudes, and feet that end in talons rather than toes. Around her neck is a chain and on her head an improbable crown. But what is most remarkable about this demon is her posture: she is sitting on a bishop and a king, both of whom strain and grimace beneath her. And then, as we study the figure more closely (which is easy to do since it is not far off the ground), something delightfully shocking becomes apparent: with her hands she is spreading wide her legs and preparing to urinate on the two worthies beneath her! When we recall that all of these figures were originally painted in bright colors, we can only imagine the effect this little scene must have had on those passing piously through the main portal of the cathedral. This is comedy as broad and bawdy as anything in Shakespeare — or, for that matter, Monty Python.

The humor of the cathedrals is closely related to their verticality. We have just seen how the upward thrust of the Gothic architecture proclaims the irreducible otherness of God, the transcendence of the true homeland that we seek and therefore the relative unimportance of everything here below. The medieval person knew that no king, no bishop, no hierarch, no institution (including the church itself) is the final good, and thus that all of them can and should have their noses tweaked from time to time. Chesterton remarked that when he was an agnostic and thought that his deepest joy was attainable in this world, he never found happiness in worldly things. But when he realized that true fulfillment is available only in heaven, he began, paradoxically, to enjoy the things of this world, for he was not clinging so tightly and desperately to them. He was able to delight in this universe precisely in the measure that he could laugh at it. Perhaps the people

of the Middle Ages could laugh at the church precisely because they took what it embodied with such
seriousness.

This playfulness is related as well to another theme
that we discussed earlier, namely, the cosmic consciousness of the medieval people, that biblically
shaped sensitivity to the strangeness and multiplicity of God's works. At the end of the book of Job,
when God finally answers Job's great complaint at
the injustice of his suffering, God takes his creature
on a tour of the cosmos. "Where were you when I
made the heavens and the earth...? Have you entered the storehouses of the snow...? What is the
way to the place where the light is distributed...?
Do you give the horse his might? Do you clothe his
neck with strength?" As mysterious as these things
are, the creator implies, the reason for your suffering
is just as unfathomable.

And God's discourse culminates in a hymn of
praise to two giant beasts usually hidden from
human eyes. We can hear the tenderness and admira-
tion in the divine voice as he describes them: "Behold
Behemoth, which I made as I made you; behold the
strength in his loins and his power in the muscles of
his belly.... He is the first of the works of God!" and
"Can you draw out Leviathan with a fishhook... will
he make supplications to you? His sneezings flash
forth light, and his eyes are like the eyelids of the

dawn. Out of his mouth go flaming torches; sparks of fire leap forth." These two monstrous citizens of the earth, which to us are frightening and anomalous, are God's beloved creatures, in God's eyes beautiful, majestic, and indispensable to the full display of divine glory.

The more completely we explore the universe, the more acutely aware we become of what we do not know about it. God's creation is always stranger than we can imagine. But because all of it is God's, all of it — even the puzzling and disconcerting — can and should be celebrated. And therefore the playfully weird gargoyles, like Behemoth and Leviathan, find their place in the economy of salvation, in the texture of creation, and in the structure of the house of God.

Now to go from the ridiculous to the sublime: the very comedy of the gargoyles is a proclamation of the deepest truth of Christianity, the Incarnation of the Son of God. Medieval people were captivated by hybrids — such as the unicorn in the famous set of tapestries hanging in the Cluny museum in Paris, or the griffin who appears at a decisive moment in the *Divine Comedy* — inasmuch as they called to mind the hybrid who is our salvation, Christ both God and human. There is something comical about hybrids, since laughter is provoked by the incongruous, the unexpected coming together of opposites. Thus we laugh when the dignified and well-accoutred aristocrat gets a pie in the face, or when a man dolls himself up as a woman, or when a sculptor presents a gargoyle — part ape, part bird, part human. And thus we laugh (delightedly, salvifically) at the odd juxtaposition of the infinite and the finite, the eternal and the temporal, the immortal and the mortal that occurs in the Savior of the world. Chesterton said that the Incarnation is a sort of joke and that "on that sacred jest the whole of Christianity doth rest."

People sometimes wonder why there is such repetitiveness in Christian worship. Why do we come to church day in and day out, week in and week out, to hear the same readings and see the same symbols and repeat the same rituals? I suppose there are many ways to answer that question, but what comes to mind in this context is that we return so often because the joke is so good that we never get tired of hearing it.

The gargoyles — ridiculous, off-beat, provoking laughter — guarantee that we will never forget the comedian who made the world and the sublimity of the jest that saved us.

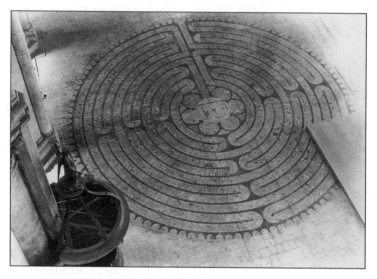

Floor of Chartres Cathedral, France. The labyrinth.
(Foto Marburg/Art Resource, NY)

11

The Labyrinth

O NE OF MY MOST moving experiences in a Gothic cathedral took place in the summer of 1998. I had spent the entire day at Chartres, seeing it for the first time after an interval of six years. It was like returning to a spiritual source and center. I made the rounds of the great building, reacquainting myself with its treasures, often meditating for long periods of time before one of the windows or sculptures. Then, at 6:30 in the evening, at the end of my day of pilgrimage, I entered a dimension of Chartres that I had not experienced before. The cathedral officials took away the chairs and the ropes that blocked access to the labyrinth, and, with twenty or so other pilgrims, I walked this ancient and powerful spiritual path.

The labyrinth is a massive circle — about forty-two feet in diameter — imprinted in the very stones of the floor about one-third of the way up the nave from the main portals. At the center of the labyrinth is a smaller circle from which radiate six petals, forming that familiar medieval image of the rose. And then, surrounding the inner flower are a series of rows folding intestine-like one upon the other, making up an elaborate twisting and turning path that runs from the bottom-point of the circumference to the center. It is believed that in the Middle Ages there was a bronze depiction of Jerusalem, the celestial city, placed in the very center of the labyrinth.

Unlike the rose windows, this design is meant, not simply to be looked at, but to be "done": one walks the labyrinth, carefully following its direction from beginning to end as a sort of spiritual practice. Indeed in the medieval period the pilgrims probably walked the path on their knees, much as today visitors to the basilica of Our Lady of Guadalupe approach the sacred image on their knees. A young man walked the labyrinth with me that summer evening and, when he came to each of the cardinal points of the circle, he stopped, closed his eyes, and stretched out his arms like Jesus on the cross. A woman, upon arriving at the end of her journey, stood very still in the center and wept. As I made my way around it, a sense of peace and purpose overcame me; I felt that somehow, despite all obstacles, *I would get there.* The labyrinth has this uncanny tendency to produce such spiritual and emotional reactions.

What explains its power? First, like the rose window and the wheel of fortune, the labyrinth is a centering exercise, a way of focusing the soul on its root and anchor, a looking to the Christ within. But secondly — and here we come to one of its unique features — the one who walks it must slow down, the very density of the path and the tightness of its curves preventing anything like a race to the center. Even the most driven people are compelled to make a lazy journey when they commit themselves to this discipline.

It is a commonplace of the spiritual masters that the deepest part of the soul likes to *go slow,* since it seeks to savor rather than to accomplish; it wants to rest in and contemplate the good rather than to hurry off to another place. For example, in the Buddhist tradition, novice retreatants are urged to spend their first day simply walking up and down in their cells, repeating to themselves as their feet rise and fall "lifting and placing, lifting and placing." And in the Catholic tradition, we are encouraged to take up the rosary, patiently repeating the simple prayer of the Hail Mary 50 times (or 150 times if the entire rosary is recited), circling round and round a few key images and ideas and not particularly *getting* anywhere. Both of these disciplines are intended to calm the darting, impatient mind that leaps from thought to thought and project to project and to cause it to settle, to savor, to rest.

Especially frustrating about the labyrinth to the

goal-oriented person is how it forces an unnecessarily long and convoluted journey to a center that could be reached in a few steps. The analytical mind knows that the shortest distance between two points is a straight line, but the soul is not the least bit beguiled by that facile piece of logic. The straight journey might be the shortest, but it might not be the most radiant or the most beautiful.

A third dimension of the labyrinth is its evocation of life as a pilgrimage. Sacred journeys to holy sites, usually for the purpose of looking at the relics of saints, were extremely popular in the Middle Ages. Chartres itself, as we have seen, was one of the principal pilgrimage destinations. These trips tended to be lengthy, some lasting several years, and they were dangerous, since the pilgrims were exposed to the vagaries of the weather, the unreliability of the roads, and the constant threat of robbers and marauders. Before setting out on pilgrimage, many people made up their last will and testament. Of course, the very danger of these journeys was to some degree the point, for they were undertaken in many cases as a penance for sin. And the pilgrimage accordingly became a powerful metaphor for the journey of life, the voyage through the difficulties and tragedies of this world to the heavenly Jerusalem above.

At the center of the Chartres labyrinth was, as

we've seen, a depiction of Jerusalem, the city in Palestine that attracted pilgrims on this earth, and the city in heaven that is the final destination of all journeys of body and spirit. Indeed some speculate that those who could not make the actual voyage to the holy city accepted the Chartres labyrinth as a substitute, provided that they made it on their knees. Thus the labyrinth, all twists and turns and convolutions leading to the secure destination of Jerusalem, was a microcosm of the pilgrimage of life.

As we make our way to God, we pass through success and failure, deep pleasure and deep anxiety, periods of closeness to God and periods of aridity. The path of the labyrinth, which carries us by turns close to the center and far from it, speaks of this unpredictability and variance. Yet, despite its myriad bends, the path of the labyrinth is one, and those pilgrims who stay to it will come to the holy city at the center. Christ referred to himself as "the way," indicating that his manner of being in the world is the path that leads to the Father. He by no means guarantees that this path will be straight or simple, but he does assure us that it leads where we want to go. The winding but sure path of the labyrinth is Christ the way; if we stay with it, even when it seems to be getting us nowhere, we will arrive.

The haunting words of the prophet Isaiah come to mind here: "The blind I will lead on their journey;

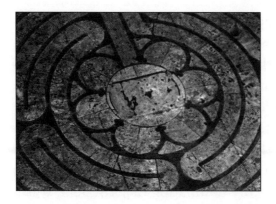

by paths unknown I will guide them." Even when we have no idea where we are going, even when we are stumbling about in the dark, God, in Christ, is laying out a way for us to walk. A conviction that was elemental in the Middle Ages and that has, I fear, been largely lost today is that God is providential. For the medieval world, God is not simply a cosmic force or a distant explanation for the order of the universe; rather, God is a father, a governor, an overseer. Thomas Aquinas says that God is responsible, not only for the being of creatures, but also for their direction toward an end: the creator and sustainer is also a Father who lures his children to himself.

In the film *The Apostle,* Robert Duvall's character, a fallen yet deeply faithful evangelical minister, comes to a town where he hopes to start a new life. Arriving literally at a crossroad, he looks up and asks, "All right, Lord, show me which way to go; show me the path to walk." Fifth-century Irish monks would set out from the harsh coast of their home island in search of an even more distant site for their monastery. They would simply allow the boat to drift, trusting that God would guide them to their appointed destination. From a purely psychological (and navigational!) standpoint, these strategies are lunacy, but within the context of a trust in divine providence, they are supremely reasonable. Duvall's minister and the ancient monks of Ireland both allowed themselves to be led by a power beyond their wills and imaginations; they submitted themselves to a path not of their own choosing, and in this, paradoxically, they found their way.

Paul Claudel uttered the marvelous line that has since, unfortunately, devolved into a bit of a cliché: "God writes straight with crooked lines." So the curving lines of the labyrinth, according to the inscrutable providence of God, lead straight to the center.

York Cathedral, England. Ceiling, a symbolization of Universal or Cosmic Form. (The Crosiers – Gene Plaisted, OSC)

12

Sacred Geometry

I N HIS *History of Western Philosophy,* Bertrand Russell claimed that mathematics — abstract, un-changing, certain, austerely beautiful — is the chief ground for religious belief. Though reductionist and meant to be debunking, Russell's claim is, I think, not far from the truth and, in fact, brings him close to a powerful and mystical intuition shared by most of the great spirits of the ancient and medieval worlds, namely, that there is a correspondence between the ordered harmonies of nature and the Ordered Har-mony who is God. Until the modern period and the Enlightenment, mathematics and geometry were seen as sacred sciences, reflections of the divine mind, and not simply as tools for the mastery of nature. Ex-ploring the harmonic reasonableness of the cosmos was a way to attune oneself to the intentions of the Geometrician who made the earth itself.

We can find this intuition everywhere in the poets, philosophers, mystics, and prophets of antiquity. Thus, the pre-Socratic philosopher Pythagoras held that the basic "stuff" of the universe is number, by which he meant balance, harmony, and tensive relationship. Whatever exists, from the planets to the atoms, has a form or essential reasonability by which it corresponds to a potential knower: this is its "number" in the Pythagorean sense. Because of this harmony, any one thing can be related to any other in a mathematical fashion, much as any point on a Cartesian coordinate system can be related numerically to any other. Pythagoras's successor Plato speculated that a similarly ordered relationship held between the pure forms and the reflections of those forms which are the particular objects that we see. In his cosmological dialogue the *Timaeus,* Plato imagines the creator consulting the forms as a sort of blueprint as he engineers the ordered universe.

We find something similar in the scriptural authors as well. We know that in the Hebrew of the Bible each letter corresponds to a numerical value, so that every word is also a number, and vice versa. For instance the letters making up the name "David" add up to fourteen, which explains why St. Matthew tells us that there were three sets of fourteen generations preceding the arrival of Christ: he was subtly insinuating that Jesus is the perfect David, David raised to the third power, if you will. Similarly, Noah's Ark, the ark of the covenant, and the great temple of Jerusalem are all designed according to rigorous mathematical specifications, thereby becoming numbered objects. Since the whole Bible was seen as coming through divine inspiration, all of these word/numbers and numbered-things were interpreted as reflections of the primordial Word/Number who is God.

In the homilies and commentaries of the Church Fathers, there is a fascination with numerology so enthusiastic as to strike us as slightly strained. Thus Augustine speculates on John's account of the 153 fish that the disciples bring ashore in the presence of the risen Jesus: 153 is the result of adding 1+2+3+4...up to 17, and 17 is the result of combining 10 (for the commandments) with 7 (for the seven gifts of the Holy Spirit)! And Origen holds that Noah's Ark is 300 cubits long because it represents the divinization of the earth, the crossing of 3 (the divine persons) and 100 (symbol of the totality of creation). Again, what matters here is not so much the details of the analysis as the tremendous confidence that these authors had in the interconnected reasonableness of God, Scripture, history, and nature.

These two strains of mathematical mysticism met in the cathedral school of Chartres, a center of both biblical theology and Platonic philosophy. It should hardly surprise us then that the cathedral itself would

become a prime example of sacred geometry and numerology. The north rose at Chartres, for example,
is structured according to the number twelve: there
are five sets of twelve medallions surrounding the
central circle; and twelve is the result of multiplying
three (the divine persons) and four (the earth, with
its four corners, four winds, four seasons). Hence
the rose announces the central truth of Christianity, the mixing of heaven and earth in the Incarnate
Christ, the reestablishing of the lost harmony of
the world.

There is something similar and even more subtle in
the south rose at Notre-Dame de Paris. If we count
up the total number of medallions and figures, we
arrive at the number 232, which is 3 (the divine) in
the midst of 2 and 2 (the familiar quaternity of the
earth): again the divinizing of the cosmos in Christ
is the motif. In order to reinforce the theme of arithmetic harmonization, the artist of the south rose at
Chartres depicted the twenty-four elders of the Book
of Revelation each playing a different musical instrument. Hans Urs von Balthasar said that Jesus came
into our humanity as a keynote, much as the first
chair violinist provides the tone that allows the or-
chestra to tune up and play symphonically. Sin is a
cacophonous disharmony; Jesus orders it into song.

The labyrinth that we examined in the last meditation is exactly the same diameter as the west rose

window, and this means that when the setting sun shines on the western façade, there is established a lovely illuminating rapport between the colored window high on the wall and the design on the floor. This in turn speaks of the Platonic/Christian view of the world according to which the forms in the mind of God illumine their exemplars here below. And like the *Divine Comedy* of Dante, the cathedral of Chartres is filled with the number three, the mystical figure of the Trinity: there are three portals, three main aisles, three elevations, and three rose windows. Pilgrims making their way through this space are meant to be "trinitized," ordered according to the number which is God's inner life.

Here we come to the heart of it. For Christians, God is not a monolith, not an undifferentiated unity, and not a "thing" dumbly at one with itself. Rather, God is a play of relationality, a *communio* of persons. From all eternity, the Father speaks himself, and this Word is the Son; and from all eternity, the Father and Son look to each other in love, and that love is the Holy Spirit.

In short, God is a harmony, a blend of voices. If we wish to name the ultimate reality, we cannot use the awkward category of substance, but must reach instead for the language of numeric relationality, pattern, and dynamic rapport. Alternatively, we can use the simple but deeply mysterious words of

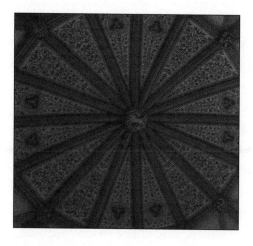

St. John and say that God *is* love, that is to say, an action and not a thing, a verb and not a noun. Aristotle held that substance is the fundamental category and relation an incidental modification of it. The Christian doctrine of the Trinity turns Aristotle on his head, for it declares that the most fundamental reality of all *is* a relation, in fact, a lovely three-part harmony.

Now when this harmonic God creates, he produces reflections of himself, since, as Aquinas says, *omne agens agit sibi simile* (every agent makes something similar to itself). Thus all of created reality, the mystics and theologians tell us, is itself a vestige of the Trinity, hence a number or a play of relation. And don't contemporary physicists confirm this intuition when they tell us that at the most fundamental level of the physical world, we find, not so much static "things" as blurs of energy, positive and negative charges in an oddly stable relationship? Through the whole of nature, in short, the eyes of faith see a reflection of the *communio* that is God, and the ears of faith hear a distant echo of the primal harmony of the transcendent world.

Music, number, harmony, balance, and tensive order — this is the structure of the real, from the highest to the lowest levels. The cathedrals, in all of their arithmetic musicality, stand as both avatars of the earth and exemplars of heaven, instruments if you will, on which are played both the music of the human mind and the music of the spheres.

Hound. Misericord from choir stall. Le Mans Cathedral, France.
(Foto Marburg/Art Resource, NY)

13

Virtues and Vices

ALISDAIR MacINTYRE has argued that moral virtues
can never be separated from the communities in
which they are formed and out of which they grow.
Thus there are particular virtues — say, courage, wil-
iness, and loyalty — that were fostered in the world
of Greek city-states, and others — practical intelli-
gence, canniness, the capacity for taking risks — that
are specially prized in the business culture of twenty-
first-century America. In the same way, the "city"
of God, the culture of the Gospel, produces its own
set of virtues, those qualities of soul that conduce
toward the great goal of union with God.

If we look in the *Summa theologiae* of Thomas
Aquinas, that most architectonic of all medieval
thinkers, we find considerations of God, creation, and
Christ, but by far the most sustained and scrupulously
careful analysis is of human moral action, more precisely, of the virtues and vices. Aquinas seems to know
that his entire theological project would amount to
nothing unless it finally encouraged *a way of life* in
line with the Gospel. In a similar way, the Gothic

cathedrals, embodiments and symbolic expressions of the Christian "city," preach the life that flows from Jesus Christ. They do so in a most colorful and vivid way, offering us, in stone and glass, accounts of the warfare between the virtues and the vices.

In a simple bas-relief on the façade of Notre-Dame de Paris, we see courage (a soldier decked out in armor and helmet) triumphing over cowardice (a poor soul running helplessly away from a rabbit). At Amiens, we find charity, depicted as a woman giving away her goods to the poor, standing over avarice, a man carefully counting his coins as he puts them in his strongbox. On the north porch of Chartres there is a bas-relief of a woman holding a shield bearing the image of a chalice containing the blood of Christ. This is a symbol of faith, that quality of the mind that enables us to believe what we cannot see. She stands over a sculpture of a man who evokes idolatry: he worships a god in the form of an ape. And at several of the cathedrals we find a curious juxtaposition: a woman bearing a shield emblazoned with a serpent triumphs over a man walking barefoot on uneven ground and placing a stone in his mouth. This is the victory of prudence ("you must be as clever as a serpent") over folly.

One of the most dramatic depictions is of the contrast between hope and despair. At Amiens and other cathedrals, we see a woman calmly reaching for a crown, symbolic of the hope of glory held out to the faithful, and she hovers over a man who pierces himself through the torso with a great sword. (Interestingly, in a colored window at Lyon, there is a depiction of a man running himself through, but in this case he is associated with the vice of anger, that quality of soul that amounts to psychological suicide.)

Studying these vivid (remember that they were brightly painted) and often amusing little morality plays, the medieval pilgrims or worshipers were being subtly shaped as Christians, their minds formed according to the pattern of Christ's. The images of the virtues were effectively telling them what sort of behavior was expected of them in the city of God, and the pictures of the vices were telling them what was opposed to the *ordo* of that city. Or to switch the metaphor somewhat, they were inculcating in them the practices that would make playing the game of Christianity possible and eventually enjoyable, much as films of the great baseball players form future practitioners of that game.

Let us look more closely at each of the virtues that the cathedrals celebrate. According to the spiritual masters, courage is a Christian quality that has both an external and internal dimension. We saw in an earlier meditation that Christianity is a fighting religion, its face set against the forces of violence, hatred, and selfishness that to a large extent characterize the world. Thus, Christian believers must expect opposition and must be ready to fight. To be sure, the weapons that they wield are love, compassion, and provocative nonviolence, but the courage they muster for the battle is that of the soldier. And their courage also steels them for an interior struggle, the one against their own desires, their own fears, their self-centered tendencies. Unless these are mastered, the disciples will not be ready to accept and carry out their mission. Thus Christians, as Paul knew, must be like athletes who deny themselves, discipline their passions, and clearly delineate between worthy and unworthy goals. Their inner courage is both the cause and effect of asceticism: fasting, controlling sexual desire, and living in simplicity.

Charity is the virtue of virtues, as becomes clear in Paul's hymn in chapter 13 of 1 Corinthians: "In the end there are three things that last, faith, hope, and love, and the greatest of these is love." Since love (*caritas*) is what God *is,* it is also that virtue that conforms us most dramatically to God. Thomas Aquinas says, in eloquently simple language, that *caritas* is friendship with God. In his great high priestly discourse, offered the night before his death, Jesus says to his disciples, "I no longer call you servants but friends," and in this he opens up a new world.

In any other religion, a human being could be called, vis-à-vis God, a creature, an adept, a penitent, an eager supplicant, but only in Christianity could the

human being be called an intimate of God. This is true
because in Christ God has become one of us, thereby
establishing a parity totally beyond our capacity even
to imagine or hope for. The participation in what God
is, entering the sanctuary of the divine heart, is what
Aquinas means by *caritas,* friendship with God. The
moral challenge, of course, is to live out the impli-
cations of that friendship, listening and speaking to
God, obeying the prompting of his voice, opening
one's heart to him, and, above all, loving what God
loves, which is to say, everyone and everything.

Faith is the virtue upon which Christianity rests
and which makes possible the symbolic and tensive
artistry of the great cathedrals themselves, for faith
is the capacity to see beyond the senses to a deeper
or higher reality. There is an anticipation of faith
in Plato's parable of the cave, according to which a
man manages to escape from a cavern where he had
been chained in place and forced to see only flicker-
ing shadows on the wall. When he emerges from the
darkness, he is blinded by the intensity of the sunlight
he had never before seen, but when his eyes adjust,
he surveys a new world of depth and color and intensity. In a similar way, Christianity holds that God's
revelation draws us up beyond what we can know
and control and introduces us to a dimension of being vibrating at a higher pitch. To be a person of faith
is to know that the universe of the senses is but the

tip of the iceberg, but a gateway, but a hint. It is to resist the idolatry of Enlightenment rationalism, which
tells us that only superstition and obscurantism lie
beyond what we human beings can measure.

Prudence was known in the Middle Ages as the
queen of the virtues. This is because prudence is the
capacity to reign sovereignly over one's life, both or-
dering one's inner powers and directing one's affairs
wisely in the outside world. It is that sure touch, that
moral instinct that renders one capable of making
the right decision under pressure and in the face of
complex circumstances. Prudence is to the ethical
life what a "feel" for the game is to an experienced
quarterback: a sort of accumulated theoretical and
practical wisdom, a know-how that is for the most
part instinctual, in the bones.

When placed in the Christian context, therefore,
prudence is a feel for how Jesus would react, how he
would think, how he would move in a particular sit-
uation. It is tantamount to having one's soul gathered
around Christ as its center, so that all one's actions
are informed by Jesus and his way of being in the
world. Christian prudence comes from apprenticing
to Christ, that is to say, moving in with him, watching
at close quarters how he lives and moves and gestures.

Finally we come to hope. This theological virtue is
related to the verticality of the cathedrals, for it is a
reaching out and up to that place where, beyond the

quarrels and heartaches of this world, there is peace. To live in hope is to be in the curious psychological space where a deep, almost pessimistic, realism meets the blithe confidence that all will be well. Properly hopeful persons are acutely aware of the pains and tragedies of the finite realm (which is why they are not superficial optimists), but they are carried by a conviction that in God's way and God's time, even those negativities will find their place in the Great Design. Thus people of hope live in the world but not of it, detached from both its pleasures and tragedies, always looking toward the will and work of God. The Christian icon of hope is the cross. On that cruel instrument of torture, in the midst of literally excruciating physical and psychological pain, Jesus hopes, that is to say, he sees things in light of his Father's will: "Forgive them, for they know not what they do"; "into your hands, I commend my spirit."

Thus the cathedrals, like the *Summa* of Aquinas and like the Gospels themselves, aid our practice in Christianity by showing us, in very concrete ways, what following Jesus *looks like*. By giving us simple and straightforward pictures of life, they preclude the possibility of our turning Christianity into a bland abstraction about simply being a "nice" person or, as Flannery O'Connor put it with typical sarcasm, "having a heart of gold." The Christian life is like a game; there is a right way and a wrong way to play it.

The heavenly liturgy. Notre-Dame Cathedral, Amiens, France.
(Erich Lessing/Art Resource, NY)

14

The Heavenly Liturgy

ONE OF THE OLDEST TERMS used to describe the Christian church is *porta coeli,* the gate of heaven. This description seems particularly apt with regard to the Gothic cathedrals, which were purposely constructed to resemble the heavenly temple imagined in the book of Revelation: "The wall was built of jasper, while the city was pure gold, clear as glass. The foundations of the wall of the city were adorned with every jewel." When one stands at the transept of Chartres, gazing by turns at the rose windows, and then imagines what the cathedral was like when it was newly built — the walls whitewashed and the windows sparklingly clean — it is easy to make the link to St. John's heavenly Jerusalem.

Yet, the cathedrals are gates of heaven, conduits to another world, not only in their physical appearance, but especially inasmuch as they are settings for an action. What is in danger of being overlooked as we have been interpreting the complex symbolic systems which are the cathedrals themselves is that the buildings are finally subordinated and ordered to a ritual action that takes place in them, namely, the representation of the paschal mystery. The liturgy, the Mass, the climactic prayer of the church is the raison d'être for the cathedrals; without it, they would be but stately gathering places and impressive temples of Christianity; with it, they are living organisms.

In the meditation on light and darkness, we presented the core of Jesus' life and ministry as the display of God's nonviolent love. In his dying, friend of the victims, and, in his resurrection, reconciler of the victimizers, Jesus judges the *ordo* of a sinful world, the pseudo-justice that is based on violence and domination. The liturgy is a ritual acting out of the divine *ordo* revealed in the dying and rising of Jesus and, as such, it is a continual summons to transform the dysfunctional "city of man" into the "City of God."

How do we see this? It is important to notice, first, the way Christians gather for worship. There is a "catholic," that is to say, universal quality that characterizes the act of congregating, and this in itself is revolutionary. People from all walks of life, from various economic strata, from every point on the political spectrum, from a range of educational backgrounds, all come together in worship of God and fellowship. (Think of those enormous boat-like spaces, the naves of the cathedrals, great enough to accommodate the whole of the society in all its complexity).

Every institution of the city of man is based, to one degree or another, on domination, "over-and-againstness," the establishment of some sort of master/slave relationship. The radical *communio* of the church gathered for prayer in the womb of the mother-cathedral questions and overcomes such violence. When Dorothy Day, the founder of the Catholic Worker Movement, was a young woman and in the early stages of her religious awakening, she found herself deeply moved by the egalitarian-ism and inclusiveness of the Catholic liturgy. Despite its baroque trappings and its unintelligible language, the Catholic Mass was where the immigrants and the unlettered could be found side by side with their more sophisticated confreres.

Once the community has gathered itself for prayer, the liturgy proper begins with the sign of the cross, the invocation of the *communio,* which is God. In this sign we indicate that our nonviolent commu-nity nestles as it prays in the incomprehensibly more intense *communio* of the Trinity. Then the assem-bly sings together the haunting *Kyrie eleison, Christe eleison, Kyrie eleison,* three times asking for Christ's forgiveness, three times acknowledging how far our way of being strays from Christ's *ordo.* As is always the case with authentic divine judgment, this naming of sin is not debilitating but rather salutary, for only the sinfulness that comes into the light can be healed.

Next, the Liturgy of the Word unfolds, the proclamation of the stories, poems, histories, ethical prescriptions and theological ruminations that show forth the new being in Jesus. How powerful this act of proclamation is when performed in the great "book" which is a Gothic cathedral, when we are surrounded on all sides by the Word set in stone and glass! What the Liturgy of the Word reveals is a properly biblical world of experience, and then it invites us to shape our souls in accordance with that world.

In the Emmaus account, full recognition of Christ comes only in the breaking of the bread; so in the Eucharistic liturgy, a complete and transformative "seeing" of Jesus occurs in the dramatic re-presenting of the paschal mystery which is the consecration of the bread and wine. On the night before he died, Jesus took bread and wine and declared them his body and blood. In that inexhaustibly mysterious act, he identified those simple elements with his deepest self, making them the bearers of his presence, the sacraments of his mission.

Therefore it is in this act and in these elements that we most thoroughly sense the new *ordo* opened up by God's love. At the climax of the liturgy is the re-enactment of this mystery: God with us; Christ alive in our midst as self-emptying love. When it provides the context for this action, the cathedral is most itself, because in all of its aspects — windows, height, play of light and darkness, mother-nave, fighting façade — it is nothing  but a preparation for and echo of Christ's real presence in the world; it is, finally, a Eucharistic place.

In an earlier meditation, we focused on the cosmic dimension of the cathedrals. This can be appreciated especially in the song that immediately precedes and sets the tone for the Eucharistic prayer. The congregation sings:

Holy, Holy, Holy Lord, God of power and
    might.
Heaven and earth are full of your glory.
Hosanna in the highest!

They consciously link their prayer to that of the angels and saints who are gathered around the throne of God, united in praise. This is much more than pious imagination. It is an intentional evocation of the heavenly *communio,* that is to say, that nonviolent plurality joined together in love and worship of the true God. The heavenly host is the icon of the well-ordered community, and hence in joining our voices with theirs we mimic and apprentice to them, hoping that their peaceful ways might become ours.

Something very similar takes place in the prayer immediately following the Eucharistic prayer. After Christ's presence has been realized in the elements of bread and wine, we stand and pray the words that Jesus himself taught us, petitioning that God's Kingdom (his *ordo*) may come and his will be done *on earth as in heaven.* In other words, we once more set up a correlation between the heavenly and earthly communities: what characterizes the Kingdom above — peace, nonviolence, compassion — we desire to be the pattern of our community here below. Now perhaps we see with even greater clarity why the architects of the cathedrals wanted to bring the angels and saints into the very structure of their buildings.

It has been said that, after the Eucharistic prayer itself, the most sacred words of the liturgy are the last: "The Mass is ended; go in peace to love and to serve the Lord." Once we have been oriented to the *ordo* of heaven, we must now go forth to transform the earth. The point is not to remain in ecstatic contemplation of the mystery, but rather to go forth as a bearer of the mystery. The worship of the church is never inward-looking precisely because it is directed to the mission of Christifying the world. Teilhard de Chardin, in one of his wartime meditations, speaks of the "Eucharistization" of the universe, the transformation of all things into the body of Christ, and it is this "transubstantiation" of society and culture and nature that we are sent to foster. Having seen the icon, we now are commissioned to act.

In sum, the sacred liturgy acted out in the cathedral below is an icon of the liturgy that unfolds eternally above. Just as the light from the west rose falls on the labyrinth, so the light from God's inner life falls on this paradigmatic activity of his church in the world. And thus there is established between the heavenly court and the worshiping community a vibration, a tensive connection, the latter becoming the conduit of the former.

If the cathedral is a body, then the liturgy — both celestial and earthly — is its soul.

Lincoln Cathedral, England. The offering of a special intention
symbolized by lighted candles. (The Crosiers – Gene Plaisted, OSC)

15

Concluding Meditation

PAUL SPOKE of the infinite riches of Christ. John of the Cross said that the exploration of the mystery of Christ is like the mining of an inexhaustibly rich vein of gold. The more we uncover, the more there is to discover. The great Gothic cathedrals are repositories of this Christ-treasure, reflections of this Christ gem, and thus they too have a capacious, a multifaceted, and a surprising breadth and depth.

In them we have seen that Christ Jesus is a mighty boat in a surging sea, and a womb, a place of safety and birth. He is the pure light of God swallowing the darkness, and he is the center around which all of our energies and powers find their place. He is God's crucified love for even the worst and most forgotten among us, and he is the Lord of the cosmos, the king of the angels. Christ is the judge, the one who throws everything off and sets everything right. He is God's love reaching down to the lowest places, and God's love drawing us beyond whatever we can see or know or hope for.

Christ is God's clown, the fool who mocks the misguided seriousness of the world. He is the path, the only sure way to walk the crooked line with which God writes straight. And he is the *ordo,* the number, the sacred reason that aligns an off-kilter humanity, as well as the keynote that draws the cacophony of sinners into harmony. Christ is the athlete who shows how the Game is to be played; he is the principal dancer in the ballet of the liturgy.

To know the Gothic cathedrals is to know the Christ in whose form and image they are. To see, touch, walk around, study and pray in a Gothic cathedral is to apprentice to the Son of God.